OPEN THE DOOR

To Clive
Every Blessing

[signature]

OCTOBER 1998

Open the Door

DOUG HARRIS

KINGSWAY PUBLICATIONS
EASTBOURNE

Unless otherwise indicated, biblical quotations are from the
New American Standard Bible © The Lockman Foundation
1960, 1962, 1963, 1968, 1971, 1972, 1973.

ISBN 0 85476 518 2

Designed and produced by
Bookprint Creative Services
P.O. Box 827, BN21 3YJ, England for
KINGSWAY PUBLICATIONS LTD
Lottbridge Drove, Eastbourne, E. Sussex BN23 6NT.
Printed in Great Britain.

Contents

Introduction

Seated in a comfortable armchair watching Linford Christie or Colin Jackson break world records makes it appear so easy. Out of the starting blocks and a mere ten seconds later it's all over and fame and fortune await the victor.

The reality of course is very different. When they arrive at the start line and are called to their marks that is not the beginning. They would not be ready without months or even years of training for that one moment. Preparation for the day that they can look back on with great satisfaction, takes time and commitment.

When the starter calls 'set', how could they respond if they did not know what to do or where they were going? Yet they are rock solid in the 'set' position because of the training they've put in for this moment. The starter's gun, becomes the culmination of all the preparation and all the practice.

As with breaking world records, witnessing to the cults and sharing Jesus with them does not come easy for most people. If you feel that you can simply walk to the 'starting blocks' and just have a go, then this book is not for you. This book is for the hundreds of Christians I have met, all over the country, who have confided that they do not find it easy to open their front doors and to share Jesus with those in the cults. I have spoken with thousands of people over the past few years in seminars from Inverness to Truro and from Southend to Swansea. The joy I have is knowing that many of them are today reaching out to the cults in love. Many have found that with the right training they are ready not only to open the door, but also to lead cult members into the Kingdom of God.

I remember answering the phone one day to hear, in a voice full of jubilation, 'It works!' I suspected that this was a new way of selling double glazing or life insurance but intrigued I asked the obvious question, 'What works?' It turned out that the lady on the phone had been at one of my seminars a few weeks before. Just that day she had had the opportunity to put the teaching into practice. She had never managed to talk sensibly with the Jehovah's Witnesses at the door until then and she was so excited. There are no five-year guarantees but I can assure you that there are many others who will confirm that it does work.

But it will take commitment. The cults are aware of this and spend much time in training. Sadly, Christians do not seem quite so bothered. Our attitude reminds me of my youngest son Luke. He could not say the word 'seminar' and when I returned from the weekend he would ask me how the 'cinema' went. It struck me after a while that this was almost prophetic of many of us Christians. We pay our money, watch the main event and maybe feel some emotion for a while. However, when it is all over we leave and nothing has really affected us.

Know your enemy

Paul tells us that we are not ignorant of Satan's devices (2 Cor 2:11). It's verses like this, that make me sit up and take notice. I know the content of the verse is forgiveness – if we do not forgive then Satan will have a foothold – but there are many other devices of Satan and sometimes we are only too ignorant of them.

Ephesians 6:11 adds to this that we are to stand firm against the schemes of the devil. How can we stand firm against the schemes if we do not know what they are? The area of the cults is one of Satan's major schemes. Through varying degrees of spiritual intensity and subtly changing doctrines, he brings many into his domain. We need to know about his schemes so that we can both be protected ourselves and help others who may be involved.

Much modern warfare and fight against evil, such as drug smuggling, is based on intelligence about the enemy. Even in biblical times, warfare was carried out by seeking to get an assessment of the enemy first. The spies in Joshua's days had a human frame and as such were very vulnerable. The spies today fly high in the sky at hundreds of miles per hour, but both do the same job. How can we expect to have an understanding of what the devil is doing? How can we have any hope of resisting, if we do not know where he is coming from? Unless we have some idea of how he will react when we move forward, we do not know what to do for the best. We should certainly not spend hours concentrating on Satan but we should at least know what the Bible reveals about him and what effect that has on us today.

The Bible shows Satan, among other things, as a deceiver (Rev 12:9). As the one who causes doubt in God (Gen 3:1-5). A liar, indeed the father of lies (Jn 8:44). The tempter (Mt 4:1) and, if he is allowed to be, a devourer (1 Pet 5:8). We must understand and be aware of how all this affects our Christian life.

I was attending a large Christian meeting a few years ago where a well-known controversial speaker was in full flow. 'We don't need all these anti-cult groups, we just need to preach Jesus,' his voice rang out. Why did he say that? I suspected then, and have had no cause to change my mind since, that it was to defend his own position and to make sure that no one checked on his teaching. However, there are those whose ministry is not just anti-anything but a positive calling as 'watchmen' within the body of Christ. They are not there to criticise everyone who does not hold their views on, for instance, the return of Christ. Nor are they there to find a demon under every new preacher's notes. They are there to give a warning to the body of Christ where teaching or action is not biblical. Reachout Trust, I believe, has been called to be a help to the body of Christ in this area.

This book will not provide you with scare stories of those who have been involved in hideous cults, nor testimonies of 'great escapes'. This is not the purpose of the book. What we are aiming to provide is an overview of what you are likely to find behind the public face of your town. From this, each of us will be better prepared both to pray and to warn young or ignorant Christians of the dangers. Most importantly, we will be ready to be used as messengers of the love of God to the people caught up in these areas.

Know your faith

Chapters 6–11 will help make sure our own position is Rock solid. This section is the heart of the book. Here we will look at building ourselves up in our own faith. These chapters are the 'meat' in the sandwich. Without this section we have nothing to get our teeth into. We cannot help others if we do not have a firm foundation ourselves. The two greatest excuses, or occasionally genuine concerns, for not talking with people involved in the cults is ignorance and fear. Ignorance of what the cults believe will be covered in the final section. Ignorance of what we believe must come first and this will be covered especially in chapters 9–11. British ambassadors abroad always need to know what the government is thinking and doing in Westminster. Without constant briefing they would be communicating their own ideas and not being the representatives of

Britain. It is no different when we are ambassadors of heaven in a foreign land on earth. We need constant briefing from the Lord to know what he is thinking and doing. This way we will be representing him and not just our own ideas.

This section will also help deal with any fear. Most have fear of being beaten in a 'Bible-bashing' contest. Many too, have a fear of looking a fool for not knowing an answer, or even worse being convinced by the argument of the cult. These fears are of course brought on by the one who is the author of fear, the devil. Knowing the One whose love casts out that fear, and knowing the word ourselves is the basis for our sharing without trepidation. These chapters are not a complete guide to theology but they will give an excellent beginning. Learning from God is a daily ongoing experience.

Know the cults

The way we express what we know is also vital; we are not called on to Bible-bash. 'Wimbledon-witnessing' produces little, if any effect. The Christian serves his best text that is almost an ace. Somehow the cult member dashes across the baseline and returns the ball with interest. The top-spin almost fools the Christian and he finds himself on the defensive, and on it goes. Occationally someone scores a point, but we seem always to return to deuce and no one ever wins the match. This, as we shall see, is not the way to win these people to Christ. If, however, we are firmly anchored in the Scriptures, I do not think there is any need to pretend we are on the Centre Court at Wimbledon. We can take a calm approach to the subject being discussed and ask questions rather than just firing accusations at 100 mph.

Finally, chapters 12 onwards will give an overview of the beliefs and lifestyle of several well-known cults as well as some ideas about how to approach them. They will also give biblical refutation to some of the most used arguments of the cults. This form of witnessing will probably be more akin to running the marathon than the 100 metres – the quality of staying-power is usually necessary with the cults. We trust this book will go a long way to getting you in shape.

There will be other groups that are not mentioned here and you will probably have more questions. Reachout Trust is a ministry that is here to help individual Christians and churches in any way we can. Do not hesitate to ring or write and we will try to provide the information you require.

1

What is a Cult?

Few of us were left unmoved by the scenes on our television screens in the Spring of 1993. A small town in Texas that most of us had never heard of, Waco, became the talking point for Christians and non-Christians alike. In the early days many started calling it Wacky-Waco. At the beginning of the siege no one had the full knowledge of the tragedy that was to follow and such jokes seemed appropriate. Looking back on the events that followed, we would not be quite so ready to make light of the people and places involved.

Meaning of the word 'cult'

First we must define our terms. What is a cult? *Chambers English Dictionary* defines it as, 'a system of religious belief: formal worship: a sect: an unorthodox or false religion: a great, often excessive, admiration for a person or idea: the person or idea giving rise to such admiration'.

The Concise Oxford Dictionary agrees that it is, 'a system of religious worship esp. as expressed in ritual'. Its second definition reads, 'devotion or homage to a person or thing . . . a popular fashion esp. followed by a specific section of society'. *Collins English Dictionary* probably gives the most comprehensive definition that adds a little to what has been noted above.

> A specific system of religious worship, esp. with reference to its rites and deity. 2. a sect devoted to the beliefs of a religious or other cult. 3. a group having an excessive ideology and ritual practices centred on sacred symbols esp. one characterised by lack of organisational structure. 4. intense interest in and devotion to a person, idea or activity. 5. the person, idea, etc., arousing such devotion.

As these definitions show, in the strict sense of the original word almost any group that meets for a specific religious purpose could be called a cult. However, modern day usage has taken on the more specific meaning that comes out in the secondary definition. This is summed up in such phrases as 'an excessive ideology,' 'intense interest in and devotion to a person,' and 'an unorthodox or false religion'. You will find disagreement among the 'experts' about the definition of a cult and so I am going to give the definition I will use in this book.

Definition of a cult

A group whose message includes either the need of a spiritual change now, or gives a hope of eternal salvation, or encourages a relationship with God, without the reality of repentance from sin and acceptance of Jesus Christ as God the Son and Saviour.

Most groups can be easily classified by this part of the definition. However there will be some to whom we will need to apply a secondary definition too.

Groups who employ methods of strict authoritarianism, or mind control, or insist that their group is the *only* true one, or who hold the threat of expulsion for any who do not accept leadership decisions without question.

This two-tiered definition will lead to the recognition of fully-fledged cults. We will see some groups who, although they do not fall down on the first area of theology, do on the second section regarding method. There will also be other groups who will sometimes show cultic tendencies without being a cult in the strict sense of the word.

While on definitions we should mention the biblical one found in 2 Corinthians 11:4:

> . . . another Jesus who we have not preached, or you receive a different spirit which you have not received, or a different gospel which you have not accepted.

Another Jesus, a different spirit and a different gospel. These three descriptions of the teaching of false apostles will be used to sum up three different groupings of cults we have today. However, we also see in this chapter the 'angel of light' syndrome, the disguise that Satan uses so often. Master forgers spend years perfecting their art for the £20 and £50 notes but we never read stories of someone taking years to perfect a forged £3 note. The reason is obvious – Satan is the same; he only ever counterfeits that which exists and is of value. We should not be surprised, therefore, to see the cults mimicking much of Christian belief and lifestyle.

Test of a cult

Just as the Bank of England has its methods of detecting forgeries we too can often detect who is a cult by using the following tests.

Use or misuse of Scripture

Are portions of Scripture left out to give half-truths or the meaning of a verse twisted to suit pet doctrines? Are verses taken out of the context of the chapter or of the rest of Scripture? Most false doctrines of the cults can be detected by a simple look at the context. An example is the Mormon claim that the two joined rods of Ezekiel 37 are the Bible and the Book of Mormon. The Bible clearly shows us that these rods are not books and this interpretation is twisting Scripture out of context.

The person of Christ

Jesus is not just a prophet or a good man. He is God and a right relationship with him is vital for salvation. Cults will nearly always downgrade Jesus or lift human beings up to his level. We will discuss in other chapters the revelation of Jesus given by the Bible.

Is salvation earned?

Salvation only comes through Jesus Christ and is a free gift; it cannot be earned. By it we are delivered from the domain of Satan into the kingdom of Christ. Nothing human beings do can achieve this.

Most cults say that you must work for salvation and need to keep the laws and ordinances of the group beyond the acceptance of Jesus Christ. We will return to this vital matter later in the book.

Domination

Whenever one person takes charge of a group, to control its every movement, you will more often than not witness the formation of a cult. It is of course just possible that every decision the leader takes is of God and so the group would follow in God's way, but most Christian leaders would not want to be in the isolated situation that most cult leaders achieve. As we shall see, this area is also the one that produces most 'cultic tendencies' in otherwise Christian groups.

Exclusiveness

Most cults believe that they are the only ones bringing salvation. The moment you detect anything that states, 'Our group is the only way to God', beware, because they are most likely a cult. Some people only find out too late when they try to leave the group. The use of emotional pressure is often applied with the implication that leaving the particular group means leaving the hope of salvation behind.

Track record on prophecy

Not one science, not one discovery and not one historical event has ever shown Bible prophecy to be false; in fact just the opposite. How do the prophecies of a group's leaders stand the test of time?

Do not be put off with stories of receiving 'new light', ie fresh revelations that explain away mistakes. If the group claims to be the mouthpiece of God then what they say must be from God. The logic of this is if they receive 'new light' that contradicts 'old light' God must have made a mistake!

You will normally have sufficient evidence to show whether a group is a cult or not by applying these six points:

- How do they use Scripture?
- Who is their Jesus?
- How can I be saved?
- Is the message one of exclusiveness to the group?
- Do they have one dominant leader?
- Have their prophecies come true?

Before we return to Waco and the events surrounding David Koresh and the Texas compound, we need to underline an important fact. Most people involved in the cults are there for genuine reasons. Some Christians feel that we should not bother with these people because they have made up their own mind to turn their back on God. The truth is 90 people out of 100 have not made a conscious decision to turn *from* God. The person in the cult is searching for the truth and has been misled. Our response should be one of love, compassion and understanding, not hatred and judgement.

Lessons from Waco

Desire to know God better

When David Koresh first presented his message to the students of the Seventh-Day Adventist Bible Schools, it was not as the Messiah. His message was that he could help them understand the Scriptures better and thus know the Lord in a deeper way. He felt that he had a special message to take to the Adventist churches and was fulfilling a God-given commission. For hour after hour Koresh recited Scripture from memory and wove together a message of impending doom and a way of escape for the few. For some, the message was convincing and they followed Koresh, not to join a cult but to serve the Lord and be his true people in the last days up to and through Armageddon.

This may be difficult for us to understand, but we have the benefit of hindsight. Today as people go through the traumas of life – bereavement, marriage breakup, violence – they became vulnerable to the first message of any convincing hope that comes along. Do not be quick to condemn such people; first find out the circumstances that have led them into the cult. Remember that most cult members are sincere people. They believe in what they are saying. To those without hope the cults hold out the apparent goal of knowing God.

Twisting of Scripture

If there is one counterfeit ploy that the devil appears to delight in using more than any other it is the twisting of God's words. He started that way in the Garden of Eden and he continued when he tempted the Lord in the wilderness. He does not always tell outright lies – half truths are more effective. 'You shall not die,' was true, but only half the truth. The Father would certainly have given the angels charge to minister to Jesus, but again that was only part of the truth.

Koresh, however, took scriptures and wove them in such a way that black ended up white. He became the sinful Messiah – a complete contradiction in terms. However, he quoted scripture after scripture; surely the Bible cannot lie? The Bible indeed cannot lie but false apostles can take scriptures out of context to make them say something else. I've heard for example that because John 1:1 says that Jesus was the word, and a word is simply an expression of a thought; it is obvious Jesus had no pre-existence. He was simply a thought in the mind of God. Again, we read in 1 Thessalonians 4:16 that Jesus will return with the voice of an archangel. Who alone has the voice of an archangel? Well then, Jesus must be an archangel. These statements may seem logical but they are not borne out when the whole of Scripture is put together. This we mentioned earlier, and we will return to it in a later chapter, because it is the crucial test.

The only way

Often linked to the last point is the proof, from Scripture, that a particular group is the only way. There are literally hundreds of groups in Britain today who are claiming this. Along with Scripture twisting, they will use direct revelation and the historical evidence of the group. Once someone believes that this group is the only channel that God is using today and that its leader or leaders have direct access to God, the rest is simple.

Koresh was the Messiah, the one who would lead the remnant through the final battle of Armageddon. He was special; he was the only one who could understand and open the seven seals of Revelation 5-8. This proved that he had access to God's way and plan more than anyone else on earth at the time.

Powerful, domineering personality

Most groups have such people. Koresh was a charismatic character who could preach for hours and, either through his skill at communicating or people's fear of reprisals, could hold his audience captivated. He was not afraid to use threats of violence if his natural personality did not work. King David of old had his mighty men to do his will. This modern David could have mighty men too.

Many cults hold their members by fear or threats. Either the fear that if they leave the group they will leave their only hope of salvation, or the threat of expulsion and being cut off from the rest of their family and friends. Or even the threat of physical violence. In this way, cults hold their members and dominate them and their lives.

The various dictionary definitions of authoritarianism seem to sum up what we are talking about here.

'Setting authority above liberty. Dictatorial.' *Chambers 20th Century Dictionary*

'Favouring, denoting or characterised by strict obedience to authority. Favouring, denoting or relating to government by a small elite with wide powers.' *Collins English Dictionary*

'Favouring, encouraging or enforcing strict obedience to authority, as opposed to individual freedom. Tyrannical or domineering.' *Concise Oxford Dictionary*

'Of, relating to, or favouring blind submission to authority. Of, relating to, or favouring a concentration of power in a leader or an elite not constitutionally responsible to the people.' *Websters New Collegiate Dictionary*

These definitions lead us to see that an authoritarian, domineering leadership will have wide-ranging powers but not be responsible to anyone. It will always want to see that its authority is obeyed without question and will have little regard for the individual. It will want to dominate rather than serve.

Mind control

One question often asked over Waco was, 'How can ordinary, rational people put themselves in such a situation? The answer is probably best summed up by the words, 'mind control'. These were 'buzz words' at the time of Waco, but what do they really mean? A simple analogy is that of a computer program. Under normal circumstances every time you hit the letter 'a' on the keyboard an 'a' is produced on the screen. Supposing, however, someone rewrites the program so that every time you type 'a', 'b' will appear on the screen, 'b' will produce 'c' and so on. It will happen automatically and there is nothing you can do about it until the offending program is re-written. That is what happens to someone under mind control. Normal responses cease to exist and a new set of reactions occur. How it is done, however, is not always as easy as writing a new computer program.

With Koresh several factors were involved. Sleep deprivation, bad diet, lack of free time, hour after hour of the same teaching – all conspired to cause the classic zombie-like response. The will has been broken and has been supplanted by the will of someone else. Not every group, however, goes to such draconian lengths.

Take for instance the group that weekly reads a book to you. The book is written from the cult's viewpoint and is liberally sprinkled with Scripture quotations. First, a paragraph of the book is read. Next a question is asked, constructed by the group, to bring out a particular aspect of the teaching in their book. Third, you answer the question constructed by the group, with the words written by the group, in the book that explains what the group believes. Add to this the group's belief that all individual thinking is of the devil and that the only truth is in the group not in an individual, and the result is that a rational individual comes to think what the group thinks and speak as the group speaks. This is a description of the training of a Jehovah's Witness, not an extreme new cult.

New light

A further characteristic of a cult must always be the ability to bring 'new light' to the group. It must be clearly documented from Scripture and show why they now believe it even if it contradicts something they believed last week. Every group has its ways of progressive revelation so that they can keep up with the times and alter any false prophecies or pronouncements from the past.

David Koresh went through several changes until he finally pronounced that he was the Messiah. Each change was a new revelation from God and a new understanding of his word.

Friend/enemy syndrome

As I watched the programmes and read the reports concerning David Koresh and the aftermath of Waco, one thing in particular struck me, and that is the number of people who *still* believe in David Koresh as the Messiah, and that he will rise again. And these are people who have lost all their family in the fire, and are even on trial for their lives. This has highlighted to me what was one of the strongest messages from Waco.

The Branch Davidian compound had a literal boundary and you were either in or out. Every cult has that boundary somewhere in its teaching. It may not be a literal compound but it will be mental or spiritual. Everyone on the inside of that boundary line is a friend. They would never hurt me or harm me. They would never tell me a lie. I can trust them totally. Conversely, everyone outside that line is an enemy. Their sole purpose is to take me away from the truth. They will deceive me and tell me lies and every action is intended to harm me.

When the federal authorities moved in to end the siege, this was the enemy coming to persecute and harm. The US authorities revealed in their news conference what they believed would happen. When they moved in to knock holes in the wall and insert gas, all the mothers would grab their children and run out. We now know, however, just how the Davidians acted; instead of coming out they moved further in. This attitude is found in every cult. If we persecute them and put pressure on them, all we will accomplish is to push them further in to the false teaching.

These are some of the main characteristics of cults that we can glean from David Koresh and the Branch Davidians. Before we close this chapter and seek to give four different groupings for cults, I believe we must show how to react to such people.

In John's gospel, chapter 4, we have the story of Jesus' meeting with the woman of Samaria by the well. This passage gives the key to how we are to act in these circumstances.

We are told in verse four that Jesus had to pass through Samaria. No self-respecting Jew would do that, but Jesus did. Why? For one woman who, in the world's eyes, was no good and did not deserve to hear any message of hope. The Jews had condemned the Samaritans; many if not all her neighbours had condemned this woman. Tragically this attitude of condemnation is one that many Christians have towards the cults. On what scriptural basis do we condemn them to hell without giving them the chance to hear the gospel of grace, possibly for the first time? Does God not love the Jehovah's Witness at the door, or the Moonie in the High Street, or even the witch in the coven? John 3:16 has no exceptions in my Bible. God loves all the world including those in the cults.

When I wrote the book, *Don't Close the Door*, I put this on the back cover.

For God so loved the world, except Jehovah's Witnesses and Mormons, that He gave His only begotten Son, that whoever, providing they are not associated with the Watchtower Society or the Latter-day Saints, believes in Him should not perish, but have eternal life. So, it would appear, reads the Bible of many Christians . . .

Many people pick the book up and laugh at that but it is not really a laughing matter. It is amazing to me that we pray for missionaries working among the Muslims or Hindus with their other gods and a different Jesus. But we will not talk to the person in the same position on our doorstep. Maybe it is easier to pray for someone a thousand miles away than talk to the person standing two feet in front of you.

Not only does God love; it clearly shows in John 3:17 that Jesus did not come to judge or condemn. That will come in the end, but for now we are still living in the day of grace. What scriptural right do we have to condemn? None. Indeed we are clearly being disobedient to God's word if we do so. Why is it that the moment we meet cult members all we want to do is tell them how wrong and rotten they are. Jesus could have acted the same way to that woman. He knew all about her and could have pointed the finger and exclaimed, 'You adulteress!' Instead he asks her for a drink of water. The woman is puzzled because Jews have no dealings with Samaritans. Jesus has begun to build a bridge of love and trust to the woman. He has caused her to wonder, because this is not how he was supposed to have acted. Cult members have been told how Christians will react. When we do what is expected and attack and condemn, we are forcing them into the cult. When we love and show interest in them as people it puts a question mark in their life and another piece of the bridge is built.

Jesus now goes a step further. He begins to show the woman that he has something that she does not have, the water that will quench her thirst for ever. Cult members believe that they are in the only true church; why should they change? The only reason they will leave is if they see something better in us. First we sow the question mark and then we put in the positive reasons. The woman's interest was roused by Jesus' attitude and words, and she was then willing to talk.

Jesus still had to deal with what was wrong in the woman's

life. He had clear knowledge, given by the Holy Spirit, of just how sinful she was, but notice how it was worked out in love. It's almost as if Jesus said, 'We're having such a great conversation, why don't you go and get your husband so he can join in?' The woman knew her life was wrong, she knew that Jesus had something she did not have, she knew his attitude towards her was one of love and care. Later she would go home knowing that something was different but not sure exactly what. A big question mark had been sown in her heart that would bear fruit.

Not every cult member we talk to will come to Christ, but I believe that in most cases we can sow the doubt and then let the Holy Spirit do his job.

2

'Another Jesus' Cults

I am going to use the three phrases from 2 Corinthians 11:4 to highlight three different groups of cults. We need be aware however that there will be some overlap and some groups could appear in more than one section.

The first group of cults I want to mention are best summed up by the phrase, 'another Jesus'. The name implies that they are close to Christianity, and they will often use the same phrases as Christians. There are some who only have to hear the word Jesus, and they will want to believe that the group is Christian. Note very carefully though that there will be those preaching *another* Jesus. The name stays the same but the characteristics and the achievements are different. At first glance it may appear real but under closer examination we can detect a forgery.

Counterfeit paintings can fool some people. Those who have an expert eye can tell in a flash that they do not have the brush-strokes of the master. Imagine that you were offered a genuine Rembrandt or Picasso and a very good copy, side by side. If you were not an expert there is only a 50–50 chance that you would choose the right one. However, supposing you knew exactly which was which when you were offered them. There is no question that you would choose the original for its value whether you liked the painting or not.

This is often the position that people who join these cults are put in. The masterpiece is represented by the message and person of the real Jesus. The counterfeit is represented by the message and organisation of the cult. Many people have never heard about the real Jesus, or if they have, did not respond at the time. Now in a moment of crisis they cry out to God to help them. A few days later there is God's answer on the doorstep. They hear about Jesus and God and about being saved. This *must* be right. They have nothing to compare it with and their eye is not expert enough to detect the flaws. They accept the counterfeit and believe it to be true.

Our job, therefore, is to hold up the real and allow them to compare it with the counterfeit. Many will not like the message at first, so there is the need for love, tact and patience. Many will not want to believe that this group, which has cost them so much in time and money, is not the true one. We will be serving the Lord and fulfilling his purpose if we persist in comparing the flaws of the counterfeit with the glorious brushstrokes of the Master.

Most numerous cults

Cults in this group are probably the most numerous and the ones that you are most likely to meet. The reason is that Jehovah's Witnesses and Mormons, who regularly appear on our doorsteps, fall into this category. Most of the established cults from the last century and early twentieth century would fall into this category too. They would bring a message about Jesus and would want to identify themselves with being 'normal' and sometimes even mainstream Christians.

How can you find out whether a group falls into this category or not? The simplest way is to take a piece of paper and on the left-hand side write down some of the important statements about Jesus from the Bible.

Some examples would be: He claimed to be God. He is the only way. He was raised from the dead. He is the unique, only-begotten Son of God.

Then on the other side of the page you would write down the corresponding statements from the group's belief.

For Jehovah's Witnesses you might put down: He is the created son of God. He is Michael the archangel. He was only raised as a spirit creature. For the Mormons: He is Lucifer's brother. He was created like any other man. He married several wives and had children. When you compare the two sides of the page, you have no trouble in seeing whether the Jesus is *another* Jesus or the true one.

Examples of organisations in this category apart from Jehovah's Witnesses and Mormons would be Christadelphians, Christian Scientists and members of the Worldwide Church of God. We will take a detailed look at some of these groups in later chapters when we deal with specific cults.

The fact that the people bringing the message may be very sincere is not the issue. The Bible makes it clear in Galatians 1:8-9 that if even an angel were to bring the message it would not make it right. Any message disagreeing with the word of God is wrong. This has to be the basis that we use and the only basis that is sound and fair.

In the complicated world we live in today we should also say that it might be possible to meet someone from one of these groups who does have a born-again experience. While writing this chapter, I met at Spring Harvest the first Christadelphian who I felt really did know Jesus as his Saviour. He and, I was informed, others had moved away from the historical roots of the group and so could now accept that Jesus had died for their sins and that they could be saved. In cases like this, accept them as brothers and sisters. There could still be differences of doctrine but these will only seriously affect our fellowship if they are on central matters of the faith, eg Jesus and the way of salvation.

To judge or not to judge

Some find it difficult to judge such people and prefer not to do it, but this comes from a misunderstanding of Scripture. We are not to judge in the sense of condemnatory judgement. Luke 7:37-38 puts these two matters together in the context of those whom we know are our enemies. Even in these cases we are not to write people off and say that there is no hope for them. Some definitions given by the *Concise Oxford Dictionary* for the word judge are, 'from an opinion about, estimate, appraise'. This is what we need to do, not, as another part of the definition says, 'pronounce sentence on'.

I will not embark here on an in-depth study of the way to judge. What I will do is underline a few examples of what Paul wrote to Timothy in his first letter.

Almost the first words (1:3-4) were that Timothy needed to judge that certain men were teaching strange doctrines and he needed to teach them otherwise. At the end of the first chapter (1:18-20) judgement is made again that certain men had rejected the faith and were no longer to be accepted as brothers. The cornerstone of the judgement to be made (6:3) is clearly the word of God. The way to reach out and win those who are wrong is expressed in chapter 5. Paul's closing words to Timothy (6:20-21) are as he began: he must be on his guard against those people who are false.

We are taught in Scripture to discern and judge whether someone coming to us has received their message from God or not. This is the heart of the warning in 2 John that many use as an excuse not to talk to the cults. What is being said here is that we are not to allow those with false teaching the opportunity to spread it in the church. It does not and cannot mean that we are not to talk to them at all, because that would make a nonsense of the rest of the New Testament. We should add that there are also very important warnings, such as in Matthew 7:1-5, that we need to judge ourselves on the same basis and not just point the finger at others. This is the way we are to live our lives in submission to the Lord and any questions we raise about the teachings or lifestyle of others should be based on Scripture and expressed in an attitude of love.

> Do not quench the Spirit; do not despise prophetic utterances. But examine everything carefully; hold fast to that which is good; abstain from every form of evil (1 Thess 5:19-22).

The fact that someone says 'Thus says the Lord,' or 'The Lord revealed this to me,' does not make it automatically right. We are clearly told not to despise gifts of the Spirit such as prophecy but we are to test them against Scripture and only accept that which is good. We must weight up and decide whether what is being said is of God or not. It is important for our own safety that we learn to judge scripturally but if we are leading a fellowship it is even more vital. The lives of many whom God has placed in our care might be in danger.

A few months ago we received several phone calls about a Korean children's choir which was arriving at churches just before the service and asking if they could sing. The group, the Elijah Gospel Ministry, would also ask if they could sell books afterwards. One of these books was *For Your Eternal Happiness*. Many churches allowed the group to take part without checking anything about them; only afterwards having doubts and ringing us.

When we put the teaching of this group to the test of *another* Jesus, we found some very interesting statements regarding Jesus.

They say that if God were to give eternal life to all who knew Jesus as God's Son the Saviour, there would be few deprived of eternal life. Knowing Jesus as Saviour is not enough; we need 'experimental' knowledge of God and Jesus.

We have become God's soul. This means 'a physical God was born' and therefore we are not people who believe in Jesus, but gods derived from God's body. God and human beings are of the same genealogy and blood. The relationship is shown by the fact that God begat a human being (Adam) and a human being (Mary) gave birth to God (Jesus).

These examples of error found in the book show the group to be a cult. The fact that it was a group of happy children made no difference to the message. Many Christians would have been exposed to this false teaching because their leaders were not prepared to judge whether this group came from God or not. Can this be really right in God's eyes?

Christianisation

Partly as a result of the publicity of the word 'cult' around the time of Waco and partly just as a sign of the times many groups are going through a 'christianisation' process. They want to be more acceptable and lose the tag of cult. One such group is the Worldwide Church of God. Herbert Armstrong explained in his *Plain Truth* magazine how the Trinity was a pagan doctrine and the gospel had not truly been preached between the time of Jesus and the 1950s when he started. Since he died, however, Joseph W. Tkach has taken over as editor and a shift towards mainstream Christianity has been taking place. This has resulted in the group moving towards accepting the doctrine of the Trinity. However, there is still some confusion and there are still areas of cultic activity as we shall see in a later chapter.

Jesus died spiritually

One teaching that we want to look at here under the heading of *another* Jesus is that Jesus died spiritually, went to hell and needed to be born again. Is this true? First we quote from

Kenneth Copeland, an American evangelist with a large following in many countries including Britain.

> The cross of Calvary . . . is where the final redemptive work of Jesus began. When Jesus cried 'it is finished' he was not speaking about the plan of redemption. There were still three days and nights to go through before he went to the throne . . . Jesus' death on the cross was only the beginning of the complete work of redemption (*Believer's Voice of Victory*, April 1982: p 3).

I should also mention the summary of an article that appeared in the *Believer's Voice of Victory* in September 1991. This further helps us to understand what is being taught. Copeland was aware that the article entitled 'The Price of it All' was controversial and he comments: 'There are people who've almost wanted to take me out behind the church and hang me for preaching it'. He says that Jesus' death on the cross only 'paid the price for the covenant' and that it was his spirit being tortured in hell by the devil and his hordes that actually 'paid the price for our spirits to be born again.' Another statement in this article seems to go even further into heresy when he writes: 'Now, imagine after living in that kind of glorious union with the Father, having to make yourself obedient to Satan . . . and to take on his nature'. The final area we mention from this article is the way he compartmentalises the sufferings of Christ into three categories. His physical suffering paid for our body's needs; his spiritual suffering by the demons in hell paid for our spiritual rebirth; and his mental anguish paid the price for our minds to be renewed.

I do not intend to give an exhaustive reply here but I believe a look at a few Scriptures is vital to show the falseness of this teaching.

Which Scripture tells us that Jesus went to hell for three days? If the answer comes back Acts 2:27, 31 and 2 Peter 2:4 we must think again. Although these Scriptures are translated 'hell' in the King James Bible, the Greek is not *gehenna* which is the word for hell. Both verses in Acts 2 have the word *hades* which is the place of the dead waiting for judgement not the place of punishment after judgement. 2 Peter 2:4 uses a word that is unique in Scripture, *tartarous*, which again is a place of waiting for judgement.

The word *gehenna* is only used five times in Scripture (Mark 9:43, 45, 47; Luke 12:5; James 3:6). Nowhere does the Scripture show that Jesus spent three days in hell. How then can we say that he did and still be teaching that which is consistent with Scripture?

We must also underline what Scripture says happened on the cross. Just before Jesus died physically, he placed his Spirit into his Father's, not the devil's, hands. We should also look at this phrase 'It is finished' (John 19:30). Copeland would have us believe that all Jesus was saying was, 'I've made it through stage one, my sinless life is complete.' But the Greek word here, *teteleslai* has the specific meaning of 'paid in full' or 'accomplished'. It is the same word as found in the previous verse (John 19:28) where we read that Jesus then knew all things were accomplished. This is not the cry of a one-third finished job, but that of a completed task.

In the Bible there was no death until there was sin; sin and death go together. The reason we know that death will not stop us from having eternal life is that our sin has been dealt with. When Jesus went into death there was nothing to stop him from rising, because death could find no sin. It may be interesting to ask, 'Why three days?', but unless the Bible gives us the answer, we must not speculate on such a vital matter.

Finally, we can look back to the great prophecy of the coming of Christ found in Genesis 3. Immediately after the fall, God gives the hope of the Christ coming. He says to the serpent that the Christ will bruise him in the head but all that Satan will be able to do is bruise his heel. This is a picture of Christ triumphing over Satan completely, and all that Satan can do is merely touch him on the bottom of the foot. This is the picture of the triumph of the cross not the prophecy that Christ would be tormented in hell for three days and nights.

We have shown that this teaching is not consistent with Scripture and therefore is presenting *another* Jesus.

Literal

We also need to be aware of those who literally call themselves Jesus or the Messiah. One observer in America at the time of Waco said that it was not the fact of Koresh calling himself the Messiah that worried him most. What gave greater concern were the numbers of people ringing up the TV and radio chat programmes saying that Koresh could not be the Messiah because the caller was.

Moon

Another example of being the literal Messiah is found in the teaching of the Revd Moon and the Unification Church.

For years Moon hinted at the fact that he was the Messiah until finally in 1992 he declared it publicly. However, it went a little beyond that, as the report by the Unification Church's own publication shows:

> Amidst the splendour of the magnificent Little Angels Performing Arts Centre in Seoul, Rev Sun Myung Moon announced in this speech on August 24, 1992, to a distinguished audience of current and former heads of state, scholars, professors and religious leaders, that he *and Mrs Moon* were the Lord of the Second Coming – the True Parents – the Messiah (*Unification Newsletter*, Vol. 8, No. 1 (Jan 1993): p. 2, [emphasis added])

These types of declarations will not fool many Christians and the initial reaction is to laugh at them. What we must remember is that they will fool others and we need to be aware that many will come, as the scripture says, claiming to be Jesus. We need also to be ready to show people the difference between the one making the claim of being Jesus and the real Son of God.

3

'Different Spirit' Cults

When we move on to the area of a different spirit, we are going to discover groups that contain people who you have no doubt are Christians; they may even teach some doctrines that are correct and encouraging. They may have areas of lifestyle that are commendable and yet there are other areas that certainly do not match up with the foundation of the word of God. What do we do in such cases?

Some Christians, leaders among them, have said that we should do nothing. These people are serving the Lord and we must not criticise them. For reasons that we have already stated we believe that we cannot just ignore clearly unbiblical teaching or excessive lifestyle. But neither must we be too quick to label these groups definitely as cults and to treat them as such. I am not sure that is fair when there are some good things about them. I believe that we cannot label these groups as non-Christian but we must not be afraid to offend and call the bad, just that.

Some groups will be easier to classify than others. Some, despite having Christians within, have clear cultic tendencies. On a scale of one to ten, with ten being a fully fledged cult, they would rate seven or eight. Others would be right down at three or four and would be difficult to define. That is why for these groups I often use the phrase 'a Christian cult.' There will be

Christians within them and they will teach some Christian principles but there will also be clear cultic tendencies. They may teach that Jesus is God, but you could also find exclusiveness in that they believe that they are the only true Church. The gospel they preach might be one of salvation by faith but there could be an authoritarian leadership. We must be clear how we define these groups and we must sound a definite warning where teachings are false.

Not a new phenomenon

Some of us might feel that we are living in unusual days but these types of groups are not new at all. A quick look at the letters to the churches in the book of Revelation shows this. We first read about the church in Ephesus (Revelation 2:1-7) where the Lord had some strong words to say to them about leaving their first love. However, we read in verse six that the Lord commends them for one thing, that they hate the deeds of the Nicolaitans. We are not told anything about them except that the Lord hates their deeds. Some say that they were a group who preached moral looseness, others that from their name we get the idea of lording it over the people. Interestingly, either way would describe groups that we have today. Here is the first example of a group of people within the church who in one or more ways are not following the Lord. The Lord's verdict is that he hates their deeds.

Smyrna (Revelation 2:8-11) had dealings with groups who were probably more akin to occultic than cult groups today. Pergamum (Revelation 2:12-17) on the other hand had their cult problem. They were not commended as in Ephesus because they unfortunately accepted these groups among them. These were people who held the teaching of Balaam. 2 Peter 2:15-16 sums up the attitude of this group. They loved the wages of unrighteousness. In the Old Testament, Balaam, knowing what

the true way was, took a bribe. His heart was not devoted wholly
to the Lord. In 2 Peter 2:10 we find the interesting phrase, 'those
who indulge in the flesh'. This seems to sum up those who followed Balaam. Revelation adds that they also accepted some
who hold the teaching of the Nicolaitans and so it would appear
that the groups were similar.

The picture I get here is of people who know the way of truth
and righteousness but who want to indulge the flesh, and who
are prepared to take scriptures out of context and twist them to
give themselves licence for doing so. God is against those who
do this, and indeed those who sit back and allow it to happen.
There are groups today who fall clearly into this category. We
are sometimes amazed at the fall of the American evangelists
and yet here we have those who are acting in the same way. If
we indulge the flesh, seeking to pamper and gratify it, we will
soon find scriptures that we can take out of context to justify
ourselves. Koresh is an example. Again, 'The Family', whom
we will mention again later in the chapter, defend their liberal
position on sex. In a live debate on Central Television they said
that if David and Solomon had concubines there was nothing
wrong with looking after the sexual needs of their unmarried
members. We must be careful not to cast stones – I for one know
that there but for the grace of God, go I. However, we must also
be careful to warn about groups in which this sort of thing is
happening today.

When we come to Thyatira (Revelation 2:18-29) we find the
cult of Jezebel. Again the cult is linked with immorality but
there is one other aspect that I want to underline. Jezebel called
herself a prophetess. There is the true ministry of a prophet but
there is also the counterfeit. The church at Thyatira tolerated
Jezebel and her message, a message that encouraged people
towards evil (1 Kings 21:25). Similar things are happening
today; how can we know and be sure about prophets, whether
they are of God or not? There are two main tests given within

Scripture: first, Deuteronomy 18:22 tells us that if what has been prophesied does not come true we need not be afraid of that prophet. Second, 1 Peter 1:20-21 shows that the prophetic word of Scripture is not of private interpretation. It is the same today; prophecy must match up to Scripture. If the church had taken Jezebel's message and tested it they would have seen clearly that her teaching was not from God. No matter how charismatic or famous or powerful a prophet is we must test everything with the word of God. If true, then we are to listen to them as prophets of God. We are to accept and take note of the command or encouragement or correction. However, each message must be tested, because some can start according to Scripture but depart from the firm foundation as popularity or other temptations arise.

In the rest of the letters to the churches there are no other specific cults mentioned. There are two other verses, however, that mention related cultic tendencies. We read in the letter to Sardis (Revelation 3:1-6) that they had a name for being alive but were actually dead. We can sum this thought up in one word, hypocrisy. Praising God when you are feeling low is not hypocrisy. Witnessing about Jesus when you are having a tough time is not hypocrisy. The true definition of hypocrisy is pretending to be something on the outside that is not true inside. Hypocrisy is described as 'the leaven of the Pharisees' (Luke 12:1), that which can get in and adversely affect the whole. The Pharisees were concerned with outward and visible things but ignored the inward, unseen, important matters. Tombs may be beautifully painted on the outside, but they are still full of dead men's bones.

This is the theme of the letter to the church in Laodicea (Revelation 3:14-22), the church that many feel best corresponds to the days we are living in. The Lord was going to spit them out of his mouth because they made false declarations. They said that they were rich and did not need anything but actually they were poor and in terrible need. We are living in days when 'positive confession' is taught as coming from God – you only have to 'name it and claim it' and it is yours. This is the teaching prevelant today. I believe these verses show how wrong this is. It is of another spirit and not of the Spirit of God. If God moves in a miraculous way it will not be because we have pretended something has happened, it will be because he has done it. If we are poor we need to admit that we are poor and in need. Then we are to look to the Lord and give glory to him. He can move in our lives and lead us into abundance if he wishes. However, we can also trust him in our poverty if we do not receive that abundance.

Touch not the anointed

I have already mentioned Kenneth Copeland and there are other Christian leaders who teach the things mentioned above. I have been warned before, and some may be thinking now, that we must not touch the Lord's anointed. I do not want to put myself deliberately in a position of God's judgement and displeasure and I believe it is important to understand 1 Samuel 24:6:

> So he said to his men, 'Far be it from me because of the Lord that I should do this thing to my lord, the Lord's anointed, to stretch out my hand against him, since he is the Lord's anointed.'

David knew that God had anointed Saul to be king and as such he would not take his life. If God wanted Saul removed, he would have to do it himself. This goes for anyone who has been anointed by God for a ministry; it is God's ministry and he can open the door and he can close it. We must never try to remove a person from a ministry that God had given. Notice, however, what David did. First, he dissociated himself from Saul because he knew he was not following God any more. Second, he made it clear to those who gathered to him why he had left Saul after winning such a great victory. Third, he was still walking with God and being used by him. I believe the lesson is there for us today. In the right spirit and in the right way we can point out the biblical errors of people who are well known and often well accepted. It is not wrong to dissociate ourselves from them and that does not mean that God will not use us. It is vital that we are aware of the different spirit that is prevalent in the church today.

This chapter will end with some examples. I am not implying that those I am going to mention are not Christians and I would not want to suggest that everything they say is wrong or of no value. If I said that I would be lying. What I am saying is that in some areas I believe they have departed from the truth and we need to accept that and take whatever action is necessary.

If an adult is presented with a mixture of good and bad fruit they can probably pick their way through it and discard those that would be harmful. Young children would not have the same capability and would probably eat the rotten fruit. The same is true in the Christian faith. Mature believers who have a grounding in the word of God could probably discern. Young Christians will not have the same ability, but will work on the assumption that if people are right in one thing they are right in all; and there is the danger. I am not starting a hate so-and-so campaign but I do believe we need to wake up to ways in which a different spirit may be creeping into the church.

I will start with the correspondence I have had with the Kenneth Copeland office concerning his beliefs, and indeed the beliefs of others in the Word of Faith Movement. Not every word they say is wrong but I want to underline just a couple of areas that give me great concern. The first we have already touched upon: proclaiming something is true in your life when it is not.

In an article in one of Reachout's newsletters we quoted from one of Copeland's books, 'Adam was created in God's class . . . to rule as a god . . . by speaking words'.

Kenneth Copeland Ministries responded to this as follows,

The full title of the publication from which the quotation in this section was taken is *The Power of the Tongue* by Kenneth Copeland. In Genesis 1:1 (and Hebrews 11:3), we read that God created the heavens and earth by the power of the spoken word, and that he delegated this power to man he created (Genesis 1:28; 2:19, 20). Mark 11:23 underlines the importance of faith-filled words and James chapter 3 advises us of the power of words, both positive and negative. The teaching of the truth concerning our use of words must be seen in the context of our submission to God's authority in our lives, so that we do not fall into the trap of wanting to grab all that we can for ourselves, whether this is power, influence, material possessions or anything else.

From this last sentence we must surely draw the conclusion that Copeland Ministries believe it is possible to obtain power, influence and material possessions by the proclamation of a word. It is, they believe, possible to 'get what you say'. Is this biblical?

They rightly say that God created through the power of the word. Only God can speak and it is done. If we believe that he passed on this ability to us then it would also be true of us. However, the verses quoted in Genesis do not show Adam creating anything by his word. Genesis 1:28 tells Adam to subdue the earth but does not say it is by the word. Genesis 2:19-20 shows God creating and Adam naming the animals. Neither of these verses has anything to do with speaking out a word and it coming to pass. However, is there anywhere in the word of God that tells us that God has passed on this ability? No. The nearest is of course the prophetic word that comes direct from God, and we know it is direct from God because it comes to pass. As far as we can see from Scripture, then, the only one who can make something happen simply by his word is God.

I agree that we must be careful what we say and how we say it. Our words can hurt people. If I continually tell my children how hopeless they are then they are likely to receive emotional damage and feel they are hopeless. However, if I simply say, 'I think it's going to be a bad day', that will not happen because of saying it. Believing that is no better than believing that breaking a mirror will bring seven years' bad luck; both are superstition.

What about the other scriptures mentioned in the response quoted? In Mark 11:23 the mountain will only move if God has told me to proclaim it. Proclaiming those words without the faith that has come from God will produce nothing, no matter how much I try to work it up. What about James 3? James does indeed teach us that we must be careful what we say, but in the context of starting a flame of bitterness or hatred or suchlike. Nowhere does James teach us that we must be careful what we say because what we say is what we are going to get.

If I start proclaiming things simply because I want them to be true then I will start living the hypocritical life. We read in Romans 4 that Abraham knew he and Sarah were past the age for bearing children but he did not just ignore that and proclaim the opposite. He looked directly at the problem, admitted exactly what it was and then looked at God and gave him the glory. This is very different from the teaching of proclaiming words. We believe that this can be a dangerous teaching – several people have got themselves into spiritual trouble using this formula.

I hope this helps those who have had personal hardships and spiritual problems caused by the doctrine of proclaiming it loudly until it happens. It has no biblical foundation and so we have no firm basis for using it.

I believe there is also one other teaching of the Word Faith

Movement that needs to be mentioned here, the so-called prosperity doctrine.

This teaching is divisive as it misses the point, that some Christians will live in poverty all their life. It also misses out the truth that to gain our life we must lose it. Prosperity teaching is fine for the few who live in expensive houses, but it is not like that for most people. Maybe God's prosperity is the raven bringing a few crumbs of food or the one meal of corn bread a day that Elijah knew.

Kenneth Copeland Ministries said in their response to me:

> . . . a large proportion of the world's wealth is in the hands of very few people, many of whom have gained it by unscrupulous means. It is in the Church's power to get hold of this wealth in order to distribute it to those in need, because the root behind this injustice is sin. As we get hold of God's principles for financial prosperity, then the Church will be able to go ahead with the task that so desperately needs doing. It is happening in some instances, but all the time we resist the truth that it is God's will to prosper us, we shall not get very far.

If it is God's will to prosper me then as with any other aspect of my Christian life I believe his words, receive them by faith and wait expectantly for him to bring it to pass. I know of no scripture that tells us that the church needs the world's wealth. Jesus taught that we are to give to Caesar what belongs to him, not take it away even if it was received unscrupulously. We may be aware of financial need in these days, but the early church did not find the lack of finance a hindrance to preaching the gospel.

Please consider carefully if the following Copeland statement is scriptural:

> You give $1 for the Gospel's sake and $100 belongs to you; you give $10 and you receive $1000; give $1000 and receive $10,000.

I know that you can multiply, but I want you to see it in black and white . . . Give one airplane and receive one hundred times the value of the airplane. Give one car and the return would furnish you a lifetime of cars. In short Mark 10:30 is a very good deal.

If we followed that through logically then every giving Christian, and there are thousands of them, would be a millionaire in a year. This is not what happens, though. Are we then to say to those who are not wealthy that it is because of lack of faith? If I believe the above I would have to say simply that God did not keep his part of the bargain!

Mark 10:30, in the quotation above, is used by Copeland Ministries in the context of money and possessions but the scripture puts it in terms of family and livelihood. The quotation puts it in the context of what has been given, the scripture puts it in the context of what has been left behind. The giving of money and possessions is not even mentioned and therefore we have no right to expect this to be honoured by the Lord. As far as the apostles were concerned they left their families behind but God loved them and protected them. They left their means of livelihood behind but God provided what was needed for them. These verses say that what we give up for the sake of preaching the gospel, God will make up to us a hundredfold. However, we should also expect to receive persecutions. This is the promise that God will honour and no more.

Prosperity teaching is of a different spirit and if we want to accept it we must be aware that we are accepting a teaching not backed up by Scripture.

I hope a look at these two elements of the Word of Faith Movement will also help us to assess other doctrines according to the biblical foundation. That these men are well-known, powerful preachers with a large following does not automatically make them right. Let us come back to the biblical teaching.

Before we close this chapter I want to look at two other different examples of a *different* spirit.

The family

The 1970s saw the rise of the Children of God. Hounded from
country to country, their leader David 'Moses' Berg wrote
several pornographic pamphlets. One of his milder instructions
was that children should be encouraged to indulge in nude
mixed bathing, experimentation, play etc but not in front of vis-
itors. Today the group has changed its image and is called The
Family. I am sure there are some Christians within it but they do
hold very liberal views on sex between consenting adults. This
is one attitude we mentioned when we were looking at the
letters to the churches in Revelation.

Nowhere, to my knowledge, has there been true repentance.
Where are those who have come forward, and not just said they
have changed, but have confessed they were wrong in the past?
Where are those who have given themselves up to the courts to
decide the matter?

The Bible shows in James (3:11-12) that sweet and bitter
waters cannot come from the same source. David Berg can write
some inspiring articles these days about obedience, faith, love
etc, but this does not make up for the ones he wrote encouraging
incest in the past.

Until there is true biblical repentance and past teaching fully
cleared up, I will always have doubts about this group. A change
in name and style is not enough; we need to see evidence of a
distinct change of the heart.

There are also areas of concern in their teaching. For
instance, in their dealing with spirits and the occult realm there
may be some danger that members will open themselves up to
evil spirits. They teach that sometimes the spiritual messengers
sent in the Bible were not angels but the spirits of some former

people of God. What makes this even worse is that they go on to teach that this is still happening today. They believe that we can receive specific good spirits who have specific gifts. Speaking in tongues is evidence of the spirit of a departed believer speaking through you. This is occultic.

This group, who announce themselves as evangelical Christians, are teaching in their books things that are not of God.

Central Church of Christ

Another example of this *different* spirit is the Boston Church Movement or, as it is better known here, the Central or International Church of Christ. This group was a breakaway from the denomination of the Church of Christ who have often disowned them.

There are Christians within this group, but it also shows some classic syndromes. They believe that the only way to be saved is to be baptised. However, it is more than that; you must be baptised into their church. Whether you have believed in Christ before, whether you have repented from your sins, or even whether you have been baptised as confession of your faith is irrelevant. The only way to salvation is through joining their church.

They further teach that salvation by faith alone, praying Jesus into your heart (sometimes termed accepting Christ), and the doctrine 'once saved, always saved', are all false doctrines. When you add to this an over-emphasis on discipleship and the need to cut yourself off from your family and your roots, you clearly have a *different* spirit.

4

'Different Gospel' Cults

Paul starts his letter to the Galatians (1:6-9) with amazement that the Christians could accept another gospel that was really not a gospel. Paul emhasises that the only basis for the gospel is Jesus Christ alone. The moment we seek to add to the grace of God we are not on the true foundation of Christ.

Salvation by works

A verse from the *Book of Mormon* sums up their teaching very well, '. . . by grace are you saved, after all you can do'. Yes the grace of God will kick in at some point but first we must be working hard at it.

Many established cults such as Mormons and Jehovah's Witnesses, which we mentioned earlier, would also be described by this heading.

As with the cults of another Jesus these ones are easy to spot. Take a blank piece of paper and on the left-hand side write down several key factors about the gospel. There would be such headings as, only by grace; through faith in Jesus Christ; the penalty of my sin taken by Jesus, and so on. Then on the right-hand side write down what a particular group believes. The moment you find a statement that shows that works are essential for salvation, or that you need to belong to a particular organisation to be saved, then you know that you have a *different* gospel.

We should notice too that Paul talks in Galatians (1:6) about those who quickly desert the gospel. We will find many people in the cults who have had some brush with church or Christianity in the past but for some reason it did not satisfy. They have now moved away into a *different* gospel.

Another phrase that is very relevant to the cults is 'not straightforward about the truth' (2:14). The truth is taken and twisted like a corkscrew. Outward signs that are not important are once again held in high esteem. In the Gentile world we may not have a problem with circumcision, but there are many groups that will tell us that the outward sign of baptism is essential to salvation. This is such an important matter that a section of chapter 11 will be devoted to it.

Unification Church

The Unification Church is found in this grouping. Theirs is a completely *different* gospel. A gospel that leads not to grace and freedom but to a dependence on working for the organisation. Moon teaches that there were two falls. Eve had sexual relationships with Lucifer that caused the spiritual fall and then with spiritually immature Adam that caused the physical fall.

Christ on the cross accomplished spiritual salvation but not physical. Moon, the 'third Adam' is going to accomplish physical redemption by setting up the 'Perfect Family'. It is this belief that leads to the hundreds of arranged marriages.

> The cross cannot completely liquidate our original sin . . . If Jesus had not been crucified . . . He would have accomplished the providence of salvation both spiritually and physically . . . Thus, Christ must come again on the earth to accomplish the purpose of the providence of the physical . . . (*Divine Principle*, pp. 142, 147, 148).

Secret knowledge

Paul dealt with this second main area when he wrote to the Colossians. The gnostic 'gospel' is that you need the special or secret knowledge that can only come from our group. Jesus Christ is not enough; there are extra or mystical revelations that need to be added. Paul cuts the ground away from these groups by stating (2:3) that *all* the treasures of wisdom and knowledge are in Christ. Again (2:8-9) he shows that all the fulness of God is in Christ and we do not need to add any vain traditions of man.

There are several groups that would come under this heading of providing secret knowledge. One illustration that most people would be aware of is the Freemasons. Freemasonry is very secretive.

Freemasonry

> Masonry, like all the religions . . . *conceals* its secrets from all except the adepts and sages or the elect and uses *false* explanations and misinterpretations of its symbols to mislead those who deserve only to be misled; to conceal the truth which it calls *light* . . . (A. Pike, *Morals and Dogma of the Ancient and Accepted Scottish Rite of Freemasonry*, pp. 104–105).

Freemasonry extends its influence through government, administrations of justice, professional bodies, all levels of management, local authorities and, sadly, the church. Some members of the Royal Family have been connected with Masonic ritual. The Duke of Kent holds the title of Grand Master.

When confronted with some facts Masons will say you are totally wrong. However, remember it is a secret society and only as you progress do you find out more. In common with many cults, a Mason will only listen to a masonic teacher and would regard all that he reads in books etc as wrong. Indeed some of what he would read may be wholly true but in much there is at least some truth.

There are the funny handshakes and the initiation ceremonies; the ways of standing and the sayings that identify Masons to each other the world over. For instance if a Mason asks, 'Are you on the level?', another Mason will reply, 'I'm on the square.' There is also some influence from the occult and there is help given to Masons by fellow Masons in business. In some cases it is even claimed that judges have given lighter sentences to known Masons.

You cannot apply to join but must be invited by someone already in the society. Still, there are over 3,000,000 Masons worldwide with possibly up to a third of these in the 7,500 British lodges.

In this country most Masons go no higher than the third degree, called Master Mason. In Scottish Rite Masonry this is the third of a possible thirty-three degrees. Some other branches would boast of ninety degrees or more! The system of advancement through the degrees is complex, with each order and level having its own passwords and secrets not known to the lower degrees. This causes the ignorance and deception of the initiates.

> The Blue Degrees . . . (craft masons) . . . are intentionally misled by false interpretations. It is not intended that he shall understand them but *it is intended that he shall imagine he understands them* (A. Pike, *Morals and Dogma of the Ancient and Accepted Scottish Rite of Freemasonry*, Reprinted 1966). (Emphasis added.)

Oaths were added to Masonry some time during the eighteenth century. Today the new candidate needs to go through the initiation ceremony of the 'entered apprentice'. He is blindfolded, a noose placed about his neck, his left breast bared and one trouser leg rolled up. Then he is brought into the Lodge, where a dagger is placed to his chest. He later commits himself to the oath '. . . binding myself under no less penalty than that of having my throat cut across, my tongue torn out by its roots and my body buried in the rough sands of the sea at low water mark'.

The Fellow Craft degree follows a similar pattern and the Master Mason puts himself '. . . under no less a penalty than that of having my body severed in two, my bowels taken from thence and burned to ashes, the ashes being scattered before the four winds of heaven . . .' The Master Mason also swears to keep a brother's secrets '. . . murder and treason excepted,' but in the later Royal Arch degree murder and treason are *not* excepted. Thus, the Masonic oath is placed above the law and country, with staggering implications. These oaths are taken on the Volume of the Sacred Law (VOSL) which in Britain is normally a Bible. However, in respective countries it can equally be the Koran or any Hindu or other religious writings.

All roads lead to God

Nothing has done more to water down the gospel than the belief that all roads lead to God. It is unpopular to say that there is only one way but that is the revelation from Scripture.

Baha'is would come into this group; they accept that there are merits in all world religions but all must accede to the supremacy of God's revelation to Bahá'u'lláh. Jesus is only one of nine manifestations of God and although all major religions hold some truth, it is not worked out in practice. The belief of the Baha'is can be summed up in three statements.

Oneness of God God is one and there is but one God for all the world. He is the Creator, Infinite and All-knowing. He is known to humanity only through his messengers.

Oneness of all religion All the great religions come originally from God, revealed through his messengers. They are fulfilled in the Bahá'í faith.

Oneness of mankind All belong to the same human family. Bahá'u'lláh says, 'The earth is but one country and mankind its citizens'.

Groups who believe that all roads lead to the same God are becoming more numerous. With such belief it does not matter which path we take and it becomes very comfortable. Many New Age cults fit firmly in this section and their influence is extending into the church itself.

Do all roads lead to God? Simply, the answer is yes . . . and no. The roads that these groups are taking lead to god with a small 'g', to a supernatural power that is an impostor and a deceiver. They do not lead to the creator God of the Scriptures. Some would call us racist for saying the Hindu path or the Buddhist path does not lead to God, but it is not being racist, it is being logical. Ask the Hindu for his definition of God and he will talk about an invisible force. As you listen to his definition you will see how different it is from the definition of the God of Scripture. Hindus admit themselves that they are travelling to a different God. The God they worship is different from the one we worship; we simply agree with them. We were told by one Christian visiting our stand at Spring Harvest that because it's a free country we should not try to change anyone's religion. How tragic; that would mean that thousands would never have the chance to hear the real gospel and find the one true road.

New Age cults

The common beliefs of the New Age Movement lead to a gospel that is the opposite of the Christian gospel. They accept monism – all is one and everything that exists is interrelated. This, however, strikes at the heart of Christian belief because the Bible shows that there is a clear distinction between the Creator and his creation. From here the New Ager moves on to pantheism – all is 'god,' or at least god is *in* everything. Everything is an expression of god and therefore we too are gods. The outcome of these beliefs is a *different* gospel: Jesus Christ is not unique and we do not need salvation in a God outside of us because we are god, or at least we contain god already. We must achieve the reality of releasing the 'god-force' within ourselves.

As all roads lead up the mountain, I can take whichever path seems good to me to achieve my objective. I must not criticise the path others take nor do I expect criticism about the way I go. I must be the one to achieve my 'spirituality' and therefore a characteristic of the New Ager is selfishness.

The gospel of the New Age Movement and Christianity are poles apart. The new ager says *you* can do it, think positively and *you'll* get it. God says you can *never* do it by yourself; give up and let *me* do it in you. Consider yourself dead and let me live within you. (Galatians 2:20).

5

Secular Cults

All the cults that we have mentioned so far have something in common. They lead their members to some form of 'spiritual' life. There are cults, though, that do not mention the name of Jesus or to base their teachings on religious writings. For the purposes of this book I have called them secular cults.

I will not dwell too much on them but it is good to be aware they exist. Often the approach made to these people has to be different. With those who have joined a cult for some 'spiritual' reason at least we have common ground to use to communicate with them the true spiritual message. With secular cults, self-improvement cults, or cults simply built around someone's ideas, this common ground is rarely there.

Ex-Moonie Steven Hassan has written an excellent secular book, *Combatting Cult Mind Control*. Drawing on his experience and understanding he gives insight into the mind-set of the cultist. In the book he divides cults into four main groups: religious, political, psychotherapy/educational and commercial.

From his secular viewpoint religious cults would be the ones we have been describing so far. He does not distinguish between those that use the Bible, eastern religions or the occult.

Political cults are described by Hassan as those organised around a particular dogma. The cults which have arisen around

Nazism probably fall into this category and we will need to be vigilant concerning groups like this in the future.

Psychotherapy/educational cults are the ones that hold high-priced seminars to bring 'enlightenment'. These we would mostly describe as New Age cults, such as Silva Mind Control, Est and similar organisations.

The final grouping Hassan mentions are the commercial cults and they have as their main aim the making of money. Hassan says concerning these groups:

> They deceive and manipulate people to work for little or no pay in the hope of getting rich. There are many pyramid-style or multi-level marketing organizations that promise big money but fleece their victims. They then destroy their victims' self-esteem so that they will not complain. Success depends on recruiting new people who in turn recruit others. Other commercial cults include those that browbeat people into hawking magazine subscriptions or other items door to door. These cults take out ads in local newspapers promising exciting travel and lucrative careers. Cult recruiters set up 'interviews' inside their hotel rooms, preying on high school and college students (Steven Hassan, *Combatting Cult Mind Control*, p. 40).

Whereas Hassan is describing the American scene, he uses some descriptions that remind me of groups we are regularly asked about in this country. Although these groups are not the prime concern of Reachout Trust, we must be aware that they exist. We also need to be watchful of groups that come close to the description Hassan gives of commercial cults.

Only half way

There are many, such as Steven Hassan, who are doing excellent work in the secular field and I believe that we can learn much from them, although, I feel very strongly that if we simply deprogramme a person, only half the job is done. All we will have done is bring them back to the place they started from, and they will still be vulnerable. The reason people join cults, of whatever type, is that they have a need in their life. At the point they join the cult they feel that this is the group to meet that need. This of course is not true, as the only one who can really meet that need is Jesus Christ.

We must help these people to cope mentally with the trauma of what they have been through. Emotions may be shattered and they might need expert help to be able to cope with life again. Beyond all this, though, the person has a deep spiritual need. We must find ways to communicate the gospel in words that they will understand and in a way that is relevant to them. We must never force people to become Christians nor must we make it a prerequisite of helping them. What we must do is give them the opportunity to have the needs in their life met.

When Paul went to Athens, he was not just concerned with delivering the people from their 'unknown god;' he wanted them to come to know Jesus Christ. This was true for every place that he and all the apostles visited. Our aim must be to treat people in the same way today. Suppose we are successful in helping them escape a cult in this life. They may be set free but one day they will die. We have given them an existence in this life but still not shown them the way to eternal life. We must be tactful. We must show love and understanding. But above all our desire must be to help these people for eternity and not just for time.

Scientology

For most people their first experience of Scientology is an invitation to one of their centres to take a 'Personal Efficiency' test. The invitation might be received personally as you walk down Tottenham Court Road or a street in your town. On the other hand you might receive the 'Oxford Analysis Test', an in-depth questionnaire posted through your letter box. Either way your character is assessed and then you will be offered courses to correct the deficiencies in your character that the tests have shown up. Accepting the invitation could mean writing cheques for hundreds of pounds over the next months. What real benefit you receive in return is very questionable.

At the end of 1993, Scientology headquarters in America won a long battle with the United States Internal Revenue Service. Now that they are accepted as a bona fide religion, they are an official tax exempt body. Scientologists have made much of this official recognition and are painting a very rosy picture of their organisation. Many outsiders would disagree, including some who were once part of the organisation. *The Sunday Times* (3 April 1994), contained an interesting article that described the harassment ex-Scientologists face:

> Police are investigating complaints that private investigators employed by the Church of Scientology . . . have intimidated witnesses and plaintiffs in forthcoming court cases . . . during six days of demonstrations outside the house of one witness, Jon Atack. Atack, a former scientologist, has devoted the last 10 years to helping victims of the cult . . . (he) claims that at least 80 scientologists have committed suicide . . . (and said) 'I am frankly in fear of my life and I am frightened for my children . . . this has ruined my health and left me with very little money for 10 years now, but I am determined I will fight them to the death'.

This article also mentioned the following quotation made in 1984:

> Scientology is both immoral and socially obnoxious. Mr Kennedy did not exaggerate when he termed it 'pernicious'. In my judgement

it is corrupt, sinister and dangerous. It is corrupt because it is based on lies and deceit and has as its real objective money and power for Mr Hubbard, his wife and those close to him at the top. It is sinister because it indulges in infamous practices both against its adherents who do not toe the line unquestioningly and against those outside who criticise or oppose it. It is dangerous because it is out to capture people, especially children and impressionable young people, and indoctrinate and brainwash them so that they become the unquestioning captives and tools of the cult, withdrawn from ordinary thought, living and relationships with others.

These words were not spoken by an embittered ex-member of Scientology but by Mr Justice Latey, at the Royal Courts of Justice on 23 July, 1984.

Active Scientologists would not, of course, agree with this definition but it is very interesting that as Justice Latey says, '(the) case is based largely on Scientology's own documents and as the father's counsel, Mr Johnson, candidly, albeit plaintively said: "What can we do to refute what is stated in Scientology's own documents?"'

What is the belief of the Scientologist? In essence Scientology seeks to bring individuals to a sufficient understanding of themselves and show them how they can improve their ways. Scientologists leave out God, church and the Bible from their definition but they are still seeking to change people for the better. Scientology is a do-it-yourself answer. We can do it by ourselves; we do not need God. It seeks to make answers to the most complex of human problems very simple, and can therefore appear an attractive way to follow.

Thetans are the life force or spirit. Originally they were uncreated gods but are now incarnated into human lives. They are basically good but are handicapped by the existence of the *engram*, which is received when the person in past lives has experienced physical or emotional pain.

People who are being recruited into Scientology are known as *preclear* because of the faults within them. They are tested by the *E meter* – or electropsychometer. This is the instrument by which answers to the personality questionnaire are emotionally registered so that the *auditor* can determine the characteristics of the *preclear*.

The *Auditor* is the representative from the 'church' who is asking the questions or giving the commands. The process of *Auditing* is to enable the *preclear* to come to a place of *clear*.

Auditing is a long and expensive process in which the *auditor* interviews the *preclear*. The *auditor* will talk about the past until the *engram* is removed. Results from the *E meter* are calculated and the relevant courses are then sold in order for the person to become *clear*. Estimates vary from £12,000–£30,000 needed to take you through the 100 steps and 64 levels to the clear state. These steps are fully described in a 1982 Scientology publication, *From Clear to Eternity*.

According to the Associated Press, court documents reveal that the Church of Scientology belief goes like this: Seventy-five million years ago, Earth was actually called Teegeeach. It was ruled, along with some 90 other planets by Xemu who spread his evil by blowing up the world with nuclear bombs. Survivors from this attack were inhabited by spirits from another planet (*thetans*).

Humans today are derived from these *thetans* and are basically good. The *thetans* have evolved upwards to humans and do not now remember their former state. To allow the full potential of the *thetans* to be released the *engram* needs to be *audited*. As you are *audited* and become *clear* the dormant *thetan* state in you is awakened.

As with other cults under this heading one of the most worrying aspects is not just what they believe but the way that they treat people. Scientologists have a policy of 'Fair Game'. This is the process by which the individual is harassed, defamed and has embarrassing information sent to friends, colleagues, press etc. Justice Latey says that 'Fair Game' may cause, 'deprival of property, injury by any means, trickery, suing, lying or destruction . . .' He then goes on to give two clear proven illustrations of this.

Many leave Scientology broken people. We need to understand and befriend them. We may need to pass them on to others for expert help, and they need our love and care to help them be restored.

The ostrich mentality

These opening chapters have sought to give an understanding of the world of the cults in Britain. It is not a pretty picture, but we must deal with the real world. We can play the proverbial ostrich and pretend it is not happening but that will not alter the facts. Legislation will not curb the cults. Hateful demonstrations will not free people. The loving, patient, and powerful witness of a Christian is the only answer.

Having painted the picture, we are ready to move on. How can I be ready to be used in this battle? How can I be safe in Christ and simultaneously be effective in my witnessing to these people?

6

Know the Truth

A preacher friend of mine told me that the word of God is like an eternal loaf of bread. No matter how many slices you cut off there will always be enough left to feed you. Probably not even the greatest saint has ever plumbed the depth or seen every facet of God's word.

The Bible tells us that a time will come when God's people will not want to listen to the solid word of God. They will prefer to have their ears tickled by the latest fad (2 Timothy 4:3-4). Paul even mentioned that people would accumulate their own particular teachers who matched their desires, and in so doing would accept myths rather than the truth.

I believe, however, that once the famine caused by the lack of God's sound doctrine is apparent, there will again be a hunger and thirst for the truth. It seems to me that we are somewhere within this transition period.

We have been moving through the days when in some fellowships the Bible has become secondary to worship and the gifts. Do not misunderstand me – we need worship and the gifts; we need to show that Christianity is attractive, but not at the expense of God's word. Luke 11:52 tells us of the lawyers who not only did not enter the reality of God's word themselves but they also took the opportunity away from others. We need those today who will faithfully preach and open the way for all to enter the reality of the teaching of Scripture.

Another problem is 'revelation teaching'. This means that a preacher can say whatever he likes as long as he says that God revealed it to him. I remember some friends of mine coming to our stand at Eurofire in Birmingham some years ago. They had just left a seminar where Benny Hinn another very popular American evangelist/teacher, had rewritten Genesis 1–3 on the basis that God had given him direct revelation. My friends were shell-shocked that anyone could do such a thing. Since then Benny Hinn, among others, has often repeated this method of teaching, even telling his audience once that there were nine members of the Trinity.

A third problem area arises when people believe only what their leaders reveal as truth. This can become cult-like and does not allow young Christians the opportunity to grow up and med-itate on the Scriptures themselves. They believe things that they have not checked out with the whole word of God. The 'end-times triumphalist teaching of The Manifest Sons of God' gains ground in this way. This teaching says that the church will be ruling and reigning on the earth and that will bring Jesus back. Does the Bible really teach that? Christians in some groups have no oppor-tunity to find out. In other groups you must firmly believe that God has finished with his people, Israel, and the church is now the Israel of God. No difference from the group's teaching can be accepted and so it's not worth studying the Scriptures.

1 Kings 13 gives us a clear warning of the consequences when the prophet listened to what man said instead of what God said. It is our responsibility to check the message against the whole word of God. Added to this 1 Kings 22 warns us not just to listen to the messages we like and ignore the rest.

Theology

These attitudes have left many young Christians without the desire to study the word of God. Some are even without the ability, and many without the foundation that is necessary if they are to grow in the Christian life. Theology has gone out of fashion. I am so glad that my involvement with cult work has forced me back into the study of God's word. As I hear each cult argument it causes me to go to find the truth. The illustration used in chapter one of the forged £20 note is very relevant. As every forgery comes across our path let it cause us to study the original in greater detail. We will then know why the false is false and more than that, we can show others why. Paul encouraged Timothy (1 Timothy 4:6) to be constantly nourished by sound doctrine and to be a good servant and point these things out to others. This verse is for us too.

E. H. Bancroft, in his Introduction to *Christian Theology* writes that theology is necessary for four reasons:

1. Theology is necessary as a means of expressing the meaning of Christianity because man is reasonable as well as emotional.

2. It is necessary in order to define Christianity. The definitions may not be exhaustive, for the objects and experiences involved are beyond our capacity for knowing, in some of their aspects. But we may apprehend what we can not comprehend. We may know in part not in full. We may know truly if not exhaustively.

3. It is necessary in order to defend Christianity against attack.

4. It is necessary in order to propagate it. Christianity is a missionary religion; it is aggressive and diffusive in motive and aim. But no possible success can attend the propagation of Christianity without doctrine. The truth is employed to produce experience, then experience gives a new appreciation of truth (p. 14).

These definitions show just how important theology is for us in our task of reaching the cults. In view of this it is tragic that so many seem only interested in the power and believe that theology is dead. Watching the old steam trains at Minehead made me think what would happen if the powerful engines were to come off the rails and charge down the High Street. The track that keeps that beautiful and powerful engine going in a straight line is vital. Yes, we can have the power today – we *need* the power today – but not just to be let loose without direction. Theology is the track that enables the power to run without causing damage or mayhem in people's lives. God by his Spirit never does anything that is contrary to the word he has spoken. After all, the word was breathed out by the same Holy Spirit and he is not schizophrenic!

There is no substitute for the word of God delivered in the power and safety of the Holy Spirit. The dead letter kills and we should not be using it in such a way. Teaching of the word of God should be empowered and enabled by the Holy Spirit, and then it will bring life. There is no substitute for theology whatever we are doing in the Christian life and more so when dealing with the cults.

I had a very good grounding in the word of God from the moment I became a Christian and for this I am grateful. When the Lord called me into cult work I found that I was forced back into the word of God. Would the earth last for ever and we live on it? Who were the 144,000? Was the Trinity doctrine created by the pagans? These and many other questions sent me back to see what the Bible had to say. If we are to communicate clearly and simply with those in the cults we must have a solid foundation in the word of God. Paul's instruction to Timothy was to be diligent and handle accurately the word of truth (1 Timothy 2:15).

Errors creep in

Errors will appear when the word of God is not treated as very important. The sin of the Israelites during the captivity in Babylon is testimony to this. When they were to return to the land we find in Ezra and Nehemiah that the study of the word of God (Ezra 7:10), reading (Nehemiah 8:18), and obedience to (Nehemiah 13:1-3) was vital to the restoration. The Book of Chronicles is often a seesaw story of good king, bad king, good king. Jehoshophat was one of those who sought to walk with the Lord. We find in 2 Chronicles 17:9 that one of the first things he did was to send out his officials to teach the people the Law of the Lord. We could multiply these examples many times over; they all emphasise the fact that the word of God is vital.

In 2 Timothy 3:15 Paul reminds Timothy that he has known the sacred writings since his youth and that these lead to wisdom and salvation. They are vital because they are for teaching, correction and training. No wonder errors creep in if we move away from the revealed word of God. No wonder there can be a problem if we add some ceremony or idea that has no foundation in Scripture at all. No wonder we fall into error if we want God to speak directly to us when his written word has already made the matter plain. When we move away from the Bible as our basis we miss God's teaching, correction and training, and so errors must come in.

Many of you will be in churches where the word of God is taught faithfully and you will be receiving the grounding you need. If not, then you might need to supplement what you are receiving by studying yourself. You will find some great study aids to help you in your local Christian bookshop. Do not be fooled into thinking that it does not matter. Remember the story of the wise man and the foolish man in Matthew 7:24-27. Unless we hear the word of God *and* act upon it we are simply building on sand. The building will survive in the calm weather but the moment the storm tests it the building will be no more. We may appear to be fine in calm weather but there is nothing like the storm of the cults to test our faith. At Reachout we have many tragic stories on file of those who felt they were strong, but because there was no real grounding, they were ship-wrecked by the constant questioning and disagreement of the cults. Every Christian is a potential mission field for the cults and eventually you will be tested, so ensure that you have the grounding to stand.

Real to me

This parable also explains why there are some people who have heard the word of God for years but who are still not growing or able to stand: our calling is not just to be hearers only but also *doers* of the word. We can hear God speaking but, as the parable of the sower shows, we can allow other things to take its place. If we are to be strong in God then we need reality. We will not be just believing what someone else has said but we will have experienced the reality of that word ourselves. From our lips will come not the third hand information about Jesus whom Paul preaches, but the reality of Jesus within our lives. Think back to Luke 11:52. The problem was that the lawyers had not 'entered in' and they were hindering those who wanted to enter the reality of God's word.

So we need both to hear the word of God and also to act on it. We need to listen attentively to what others are saying but then also know the work of the Holy Spirit making that message real in our lives. Without these steps we are not allowing Scripture to have full effect in our lives. This is probably the one area in which we need to be selfish. Paul told Timothy to pay attention to himself first and then give out to others (1 Timothy 4:16). If the word of God is not worked out in reality in our lives then we will not be much help to others.

What about me?

In the area of the cults, probably the most important question we need answered from Scripture is, am I safe when dealing with them? The Bible is clear on this matter but if we have never seen it then we will have doubts and fears. These doubts and fears, in Satan's usual way will be based on fiction rather than fact. However, once we have the solid ground of the word of God under our feet we can be strong.

We need to go back to the beginning. The foundation for our position as we seek to help those who have been blinded by Satan is found in Genesis 1:1; 'In the beginning God . . .'. No one else was there, no other heavenly creation and certainly no earthly creation. God was there alone! I often say that one of the greatest helps in spiritual warfare is to picture a totally blank piece of paper with just one word written at the top, God. He is all-supreme and no other being in heaven or on earth can match him. He is the only one who is omnipresent, everywhere, all the time. He is the only one who knows everything and can control everything. Some Christians want to give these attributes to Satan but his position is seen when we read Psalm 148:1-6; God created all heavenly things, including the angels. In other words, God created the angel who was to rebel and become Satan. God is clearly more powerful than Satan ever was. Satan's fall is recorded in Isaiah 14:12-15 and Ezekiel 28:12-19. No one can lift their hand against God and win.

After the heavenly creation we read that God created the earth. The heavenly creation was supernatural but the human realm was natural. Clearly then, as a human I am not stronger than Satan because he is heavenly and I am earthly. No wonder he can deceive and manipulate this human race; he is greater than we are! But remember, before you start panicking, that Satan is not greater than God. As I give my will over to Christ and allow him to be Lord, he takes control. Satan no longer has to contend with a mere human being but Christ in me. Is Satan stronger than Christ in me? No! As Christians we are stronger because Satan is subject to Christ. James 4:7 puts it in a nutshell. This verse does not just say that if we resist the devil he will flee; that would not be scriptural! What it does say is 'Submit yourselves . . . to God. Resist the devil, and he will flee from you'. The promise of God's word is that as I am subject to Christ in my life the devil must flee as I resist him. Not because I am great but because Christ in me has already won the victory. This is our position in Christ. If this is reality to us then we can approach the cults not with fear and trepidation but with that humble assurance of who we are in Christ.

Over to you

Do be encouraged to find out the joys of studying the word of God for yourself. First, it will build you up and you will learn what God wants to reveal to you. Secondly, you will be able to communicate what you find to others. This is the way to study Scripture – allow God to speak to you so that you can speak to others.

Seeing a truth from God's word and allowing God to make it real in our lives is step one; we then need to express it with the right attitude. Hitting someone over the head with a 'heavy word' is not the way. The word of God is described in Ephesians 6 as the 'sword of the Spirit'. He is the one who will enable us to use the Scriptures with tact and finesse but without losing its power. He is the one who will enable us to build bridges and yet still convey what God thinks about the cult group. It is not always easy; we need to look at the work of the Holy Spirit in our preparation for reaching out to the cults.

7

Know the Life

It had been a traumatic few weeks for the small band of followers. Their leader had been killed and they had to hide because
of the persecution. Feeling scared and vulnerable, they had seen
their leader walk through the wall of their upstairs room several
days after he had died, and eat with them. Now they were standing on a hillside talking to two angels after they had seen their
leader rising into heaven and out of sight through the clouds. No
one would ever believe them!

However, that was not the immediate worry of this small
group; it was Jesus' last words that had rooted them to the spot.
Trying to find out exactly what would happen, and when they
would be free from Roman occupation, they had asked him
about the setting up of his kingdom. He had mentioned it often
but surely it was now or never. Maybe the latter, because
according to his answer that was not for them to know, but still
what he said caused consternation.

When the Holy Spirit came upon them, they would be his
witnesses. They would have no option, other than to be a good
witness or a bad witness. When the Lord sent the Holy Spirit to
be with them he would testify of Jesus and so their lives would
be bound up with him. Yet there was more: 'You will be my
witnesses in Jerusalem . . .'. That was a little bit frightening
because of all the persecution that had been going on, although

70

at least they could speak to people who understood them and would probably be sympathetic. '. . . and in all Judea' was a challenge, but they would still be dealing with people they would feel at home with. Then the bombshells started to drop: '. . . and in Samaria'. That could not be, because Jews have no dealings with the Samaritans. How on earth can we ever tell *them*? And if we do, what will the people in Jerusalem say? Still there was worse: '. . . and to the ends of the earth.' That was in the hands of the Gentiles. It would be bad enough speaking to the Samaritans, but witnessing to the Gentiles as well . . . !

I hope you get the picture of the shock that these disciples must have felt. Nothing had ever happened like the events that they witnessed and now they were being told to do things that no Jew had ever done before. It is a lesson that we need to learn when dealing with the cults. We may feel that many cults are just like the Samaritans to the Jews – we have no dealings with *them*. We may feel they are like the Gentiles, those who do not deserve to receive the gospel of grace. But the fact remains that we have been chosen to be witnesses to them. The only option will be whether we will witness to them of the true love and grace of God, or show them hatred and persecution. Either way we will be witnesses, and either way they will react to what they see and hear from our witness.

God's enabler

The Holy Spirit is part of the Godhead and he needs to be treated and respected as God. We must never lose sight of the fact of who he is and what the Scriptures reveal about him. Ephesians 1 gives us a picture of the Godhead. Verses 3–4 show us that the Father is the originator; verses 4–12 show that Jesus is the one who makes it all possible; verses 13–14 show that the Holy Spirit is the one who equips and makes it real within the lives of God's children. That is his ministry to us today. The fullness of our salvation has not yet been revealed but it will come because of the Holy Spirit within our lives.

We may not always feel that we are filled to overflowing; the widow who spoke to Elisha certainly did not (2 Kings 4). She had to be reminded that she had the small jar of oil tucked away in some dark cupboard. Then she was encouraged to use it under the direction of Elijah, and what a miracle! The small amount of oil became a house full. Oil in the Old Testament is a picture of the Holy Spirit. Sometimes we only have a small amount tucked away somewhere but we need to pour it out at the Lord's command. We too will find it will keep pouring until the need is met.

The Holy Spirit also distributes gifts as he pleases (1 Corinthians 12:11). These enable us to bring the reality of the life of God to people in this world. Tapping into God's knowledge is not just so we can do some spiritual party trick, but so that God can reveal something that will bring glory to his name. Speaking in prophecy is not just so you will know which job to go after or home to buy. Prophecy is God speaking directly into people's situations and affecting them by his life. I would not say that it is *essential* to know the gifts of the Holy Spirit when speaking to cult members, but we should note that usually they are a tremendous asset.

Some cults say that the gifts of the Holy Spirit are not for today; they were only necessary to see the early church established or until that which is perfect, the Bible, came into being. This last thought comes from 1 Corinthians 13:10 which says that when that which is perfect comes, the gifts that are partial will cease. But, what is 'that which is perfect' and, more to the point, has it come? As great as the Bible is, I do not believe it is that which is perfect. There is still a greater revelation for us when God sets up his kingdom and that to which the Bible points forward will be a reality. When we see the Lord face to face we will not need the gifts, but until then they reveal God to the people, and we should be seeking the Lord to release them through us for ministry to the cults – among other things.

Love, patience and faithfulness are often qualities needed when dealing with cult members and these are shown to be fruits of the Holy Spirit. We may have a measure of these things in our own personality but eventually that will be exhausted. Remember, though, God's great enabler never tires and he can continue to provide these qualities beyond our own resources. Welcome the Holy Spirit into your life and give him the opportunity to produce the fruits. Fruit is not just for you to hold and say how wonderful it looks. Fruit is to be tasted. Those in the cults will see the fruit of the Holy Spirit in you and will want to taste and see what it is.

We need the ministry of the Holy Spirit if we are to talk to the cults. He is the one who provides the power for the steam train to run on the track of God's word. If you have not taken enough notice of the third person of the Trinity until now, do take this opportunity to seek God. Ask the Lord that he will give you a greater awareness of this person of the Godhead and will reveal his vital work in your life. Please be encouraged by Luke 11:13 where we are told that the Father will give the Holy Spirit to those who ask. We certainly needed to know the work of the Holy Spirit when we first accepted Christ, but there is also an ongoing ministry for every day of our Christian lives. Let us ask God to minister through us to others.

Let us now look at some specific ways that he will help us as we prepare to reach out to those in the cults.

The changing work of the Holy Spirit

If you are perfect you have my permission to skip this section. All still here? Good! Most Christians are aware that they are not

perfect and that changes are needed. In the area of communicating to the cults I find I need the Holy Spirit to make several
things real in my life. He also has to change the way I do things.
I can look back in my life to at least two occasions where God
has had to bring me down to the ground. We cannot be used if
we think we are the greatest thing since Balaam's ass. We
cannot be used if we just go blundering on like Elijah running
away from that still small voice. Even with the earthquake,
thunder and lightning going on around us, we need the peace of
God within to enable us to listen. The Holy Spirit needs to teach
us these lessons. Sometimes the lessons are hard because we are
determined to go our own way. The Holy Spirit brings a 'soft-
ness' to our personalities although we are not 'softies'. He
brings a gentleness in the way we say the hardest things. These
qualities are vital as we get ready to speak to the cult member.

James 1:19 highlights the pre-eminent quality of
communication that we need the Holy Spirit to make real in our
lives – and this has nothing to do with speaking. We are told to
be quick to hear and slow to speak. So much can be accomplished as we listen to people telling us about themselves. The
Holy Spirit can give us an insight into the character behind the
words. If we have our pat answer ready and two minutes after
the cultist has started, we are telling him the way to solve all his
problems, I doubt if we are under the guidance of the Holy
Spirit. Many are ready to shout, 'Jesus is the answer', before
anyone has asked a question. Many have learnt the appropriate
Scripture and the appropriate counsel for each situation they
come across. This does not work. We are not talking about static
situations but about living people and each person will be different. We need to allow the Holy Spirit to teach us to be quiet and
let him do the talking when he is ready.

We are not to condone wrong attitudes and beliefs of cultists,
yet at the same time we are not to condemn them, for what may
be genuine reasons, for being in the cult. We must not put stan-

dards on them that God has not put on us. Hebrews 4:14–5:10 shows us that our High Priest can both understand us and sympathise with our weaknesses. These may not be qualities that come naturally to us, but they are qualities that the Holy Spirit can reveal in us. They are also vital qualities if we are truly going to help people be set free.

Victims of the cults need to be shown lots of love and care. They need to experience compassion and restoration. Our care for people will often have to go beyond just the initial 'preaching of the gospel'. If they come to our church we may be helping them for many months. They may have said and done things of which they are now ashamed, or other Christians may have condemned them for what they have done. A few platitudes are not the answer. We need to meditate on Jesus' treatment of Peter in John 21. There are clear indications that Jesus was deliberately reminding Peter – and maybe the others – of the night of the betrayal. The fire will have reminded Peter of the fire he stood beside and denied his Lord. (Interestingly the Greek word for fire in those two instances is the same and these are the only times that word is used in Scripture.) Three times the Lord asked Peter if he loved him, reminding Peter of the three denials. Jesus did not do it to condemn but rather to show the restoration work that God wanted to do in Peter's life. Cult members have probably said and done many things that they now regret. Many may have even misrepresented Christ and persecuted Christians – as Paul did. And just as the Lord received and restored Peter and Paul, so we are to welcome and help these ex-cult members.

I cannot emphasise this quality of the Holy Spirit enough. John 16:8 tells us that the Holy Spirit will convict not condemn. As those filled with the Holy Spirit we will not have a ministry of condemnation, but the Spirit will move through us to convict the sinner. Condemnation says, 'You have sinned and you have had it'! Conviction says, 'You have sinned and this is the way out.' The Holy Spirit will convict these people but not condemn them.

Communication of the Holy Spirit

We should continually be learning lessons about the Holy Spirit's enabling, although I'm sure we will never get perfect in one area before he moves us on to another. While our education continues, we can begin to learn about the next stage too. Having come to recognise at least the basics in our character that need to be changed, having 'got into negotiation' with God to do the work by the Holy Spirit, we can now look at the next step. In the last section we talked about our inward attitudes to these people and the need to be silent and listen. Now we need to look at what we are to say when we open our mouth.

In our seminars at Reachout Trust we teach various presentations that can be used with the different cults. We give no five-year guarantees and we also urge people not to rely just on the plans; it is the Holy Spirit who will convict a person of what is wrong and what is right. If we ever get to the stage of thinking that pointing out a specific verse in a particular way will mean that a person will come to Christ, we are going to be disappointed. The purpose of the presentations is to offer the best way of sharing the gospel with the cultists. Their minds only think in certain ways and they have all sorts of protective mechanisms to prevent any serious questions getting through to them.

In the old days an army would use a battering ram to make an opening into a fortified city so that it could be taken from the inside. Our presentation is a similar breaking down of the barrier to get inside a person's mind. We want to make them look at something in a different light so that all their standard alarms and protection mechanisms are switched off. With their power source disconnected, a new source can come on line and the Holy Spirit will have a way into their life. But again I would urge you to use presentations but not rely on them. Rely on the fact that the Holy Spirit can use what is being said; he can bring a freshness to a message that these people have been told is not for them.

Teaching of the Holy Spirit

John 16:13 tells us clearly that it is the work of the Holy Spirit to lead into all truth. He may use us but it is his job and we can trust him to do it in his time and his way. I remember an incident with one of the first Jehovah's Witnesses that I led to the Lord. She was coming very close to receiving Christ as her Saviour but had a real problem about the Trinity. A succinct and helpful answer was needed. I felt the Holy Spirit prompt me to say, 'Don't worry about it; it doesn't matter for now.' Although I said it, feeling it was from the Lord, I did worry about it on the way home. I only stopped worrying when I remembered that on the night I came to Christ I did not believe or understand the Trinity. I am not even sure if I knew that Jesus was God! At that time it did not matter. What did matter was that I knew that Jesus was God's sacrifice for sin and that if I truly repented I could be saved. A few weeks later, after this woman had come to Christ, I was greeted with a broad smile when I knocked on her door. She told me excitedly that she had been reading her Bible and had seen the Trinity on every page!

I learnt some lessons from this incident. First, it is the Holy Spirit's job to lead us into all truth. He has been doing it far longer and does it far better than we ever can. Commit the people you are dealing with firmly into his hands. Secondly, we are not to put conditions on people that God does not put on us. He does not demand that we fully understand the Trinity before we accept him. We should not expect every cult member to get all their theology right before they repent and receive Christ.

Sometimes it will take many months or years to do all of that. This leads me to the third lesson; it is according to the Holy Spirit's timing and plans that these things are dealt with. My job is to encourage cult members to trust themselves fully to God. This gives the Holy Spirit the opportunity to work at his pace, and in his way, within their lives.

Leading of the Holy Spirit

Under this final heading I want to emphasise something we mentioned earlier in the chapter – the still small voice within. Some of you will never have experienced a word of knowledge, but that does not mean that you will never will. Some may think they have never made a prophetic statement that has brought the reality of God directly into the life of someone else, but there is always a first time. These gifts of the Holy Spirit are often stereotyped in our minds and that is partly why we do not experience them. We may think you have to be a preacher at the end of the meeting to get a word of knowledge about those who need healing or deliverance. The prophetic word must come in a booming voice, go on for several minutes and end or begin with, 'Thus says the Lord'. These gifts may come like this, but that is not the only way. If we restrict them in this manner then we could be missing out on knowing the Holy Spirit at work in our lives.

Having learned all the rights and wrongs of what to do with cult members, and having learnt a great presentation and underlined all the relevant Scriptures, you may feel you are ready and nothing is going to stop you. You start at A and whatever happens you are determined to plough through to Z. There may be times when that is right, but please ensure that there is enough trust in the Lord to allow the Holy Spirit to whisper something to you. He may reveal to you that this cultist has a doubt over one aspect of the faith and that you should mention that subject. Don't think you can't, simply because this is not what you have prepared. The Lord may want to speak directly through you.

How will you hear or see these words? Probably not by someone writing them in the sky or by a booming voice in your ear. It will not be an audible voice at any level, but just a feeling within your spirit. Respond to that small voice as Elijah did. You will be nervous and there will probably be times when you make mistakes, but there will be other times when you see the Holy Spirit working. I remember spending several hours with two Jehovah's Witnesses and getting absolutely nowhere. It was about 1 am and I was just about to go when I had a feeling that I should introduce a particular scripture that I never usually mention to Witnesses. I will never forget the look on the face of one of them. It was just as if he had been hit in the stomach by a heavyweight boxing champion. I knew that at that point the Holy Spirit spoke to him.

We have looked at two hurdles in our preparation, knowing the truth of the word of God and knowing the life of the Holy Spirit, but there is still a further hurdle, knowing the way of prayer. Without prayer we will have little or no success in seeing cult members set free.

8

Know the Way

One day Jesus was praying in a certain place. When he finished, one of his disciples said to him, 'Lord, teach us to pray, just as John taught his disciples.'

From the incident that takes place at the beginning of Luke 11:1, we can draw two conclusions. First, one of the key areas in discipleship is prayer. John had taught his disciples to pray and now Jesus' disciples wanted him to do the same. Secondly, the way that Jesus prayed alerted the disciples to the fact that they did not really know how to pray. Some of these men had been with John and would have learned something, but as they listened and watched Jesus they knew there was more that they should learn.

What is prayer?

First, prayer is not directed towards other people, it is for God; Matthew 6:5-6 makes this clear. We should not be trying to use the most flowery language; in fact we should be using the most practical language possible. Prayer is bringing our requests and petitions to God, with genuine heartfelt words and an expectation of his hearing and answering. Let us beware of prayer that is written for people to hear and has no belief behind it that the Lord will even listen, let alone answer.

Matthew 6:7 goes on to show that prayer does not come from the mind but from the spirit. Prayer is something that God inspires and not simply something which comes from good man-made phrases. Luke 18:9-14 records the story of the two men in the temple and it illustrates this point clearly. The Pharisee, who it is said trusted in himself and told God how great a man he was, received nothing. On the other hand the poorer man, who knew his true condition and cried from his heart to God, received in abundance.

Matthew 6:7 does not put the emphasis just on the repetition but on the *meaningless* repetition. We shall see later that persistence, even using the same words, can be of God, but vain repetition week after week does not achieve anything. Words that come out of our own proud attitude are not received. God always resists the proud but gives grace and responds to the humble.

Probably the most helpful picture of prayer is a circle. The Lord sits at the top of the circle and begins to express his will and the circle begins to be drawn. We sit at the bottom of the circle and if we are listening for the voice of the Lord and respond we will pray out from God's heart. The circle is then completed and returns fulfilled to God. Daniel is an example of this. He realised the will of God was for the people to go back to their land after the captivity and he knew the time was right. This did not mean that he just sat back and said, 'That is fine. God has said it. He will do it'. He completed the circle by praying three times a day until the thing was done. There will be people in the cults whom God wants to reach and he will remind us of them so we can pray for as long as necessary. Circumstances will be revealed to us and the Lord will show what he wants to do. We need to co-operate with him and pray the matter to a conclusion.

A similar picture is seen in Matthew 7:7: ask . . . seek . . . knock. We first *ask* the Lord what is in his heart and he tells us. We then *seek* his will on the matter until we feel we are clear and we have found what he wants to do. Finally, we *knock* specifically on the door and the Lord will open the way to us. In all these things we are co-operating with God. He begins and we follow his will.

> This is the confidence we have in approaching God: that if we ask anything according to his will, he hears us. And if we know that he hears us – whatever we ask – we know that we have what we asked of him (1 John 5:14-15).

Prayer is an adventure of listening to the Lord's voice and having the privilege of working with him to see his will worked out on the earth.

Prayer makes the way

The answer that Jesus gave to the disciples in Luke 11 made it clear that one main purpose of prayer is to bring the kingdom of God to earth. We have nothing in ourselves of any lasting value to give to cult members. At the same time many of these people have been heavily influenced by satanic power and we cannot break this by ourselves. The only way that we are going to help them is by seeing God move in power, and prayer is the key to that.

I have been made aware of many pitfalls in this ministry and I believe we need to have a clear understanding of what the Lord teaches about prayer and how we should be praying. First because prayer is making the way for the Lord, it should be going on regularly before meeting with individuals. Many people in the cults will not want you to pray with them because they will feel that you are talking to Satan. Do not be worried about this. And don't feel that you must go through the routine of praying during the meeting. Why cause these people more problems? We are trying to build bridges to them, not bang them over the head.

One visitor to our stand at Spring Harvest told me how his pastor had taught that you should not discuss scriptures with these people when they call at the door. You must not talk – you must simply bind the spirits within them. So the next time the Jehovah's Witnesses called, he bound the theological spirits that were in them. But before he had finished praying they were half way down the street – nothing had been achieved. The Witnesses would now be convinced that all Christians were of the devil. We will need to pray strongly for them, but before they arrive and after they leave. If any prayer goes on while they are there it will normally be silent; God still hears!

If we look at Jesus' life we see how he handled this matter of prayer. He did not stop and pray before each sermon he gave or before each person was brought to him for ministry. He had been praying the night before or in the early morning and he was ready to minister. It can just be superstition to want to start every meeting with prayer. If you have been praying beforehand you are ready in the Lord to minister and praying in front of the cultist may simply be a hindrance.

A spiritual battle

We must never forget that we are in a battle with our spiritual enemy, *not* with the person we are talking to. This means that the warfare should be undertaken in the spiritual realms and not with the people concerned. The condition of the cultists we are dealing with is aptly expressed by 2 Corinthians 4:4, '. . . the god of this world has blinded the minds . . .'. If we are to see them released, then the battle of the mind has to be won.

Pray constantly for the cult members in your area. Pray

especially when you know people are coming; and pray for people you know by name. If they live next door lay hands on the wall but do not walk round the house six times if it's semi-detached (remember Jericho!). I remember a local prayer meeting a few years ago. The house at the bottom of the garden belonged to a Jehovah's Witness elder and the Lord gave us the desire to pray very strongly for him. The following Saturday I noticed some Witnesses in our road and as they never knock at my door I went out to mend the garden gate! A friendly good morning stopped them in their tracks and before long we were sitting in my front room. After an hour or more of good conversation I asked for the address to send them some more information. I nearly shouted 'Hallelujah!' when one of them told me he lived in the very house we had been praying for. I still believe the Lord wants to work in that family.

We also need to pray that the battle already won in the heavenly places will be worked out on the earth. Pray that cult members will be open to receiving the truth of Scripture. If you feel inadequate for the battle be encouraged by the story of David and Goliath in 1 Samuel 17. David was the smallest and youngest in his house but God saw his heart. The secret of David's victory was not what happened five minutes before he met Goliath but what had been going on in the fields with the sheep. David had learned to trust the Lord, and the lion or the bear held no fear for him. They could not steal any sheep when the Lord was in control. This enemy was no different, and the same lessons of trust the Lord had taught him in the wilderness came into play here. He refused to use Saul's armour that he had not tested, but instead trusted the weapons that he had learned to use in the wilderness.

Be encouraged. Even if you feel you are the smallest and the least, God wants to teach you lessons now that you can use in his warfare later. Learn to trust him where you are now and he will use you in greater ways in the days ahead. Learn to use things that are real to *you* and that have been tried and tested outside the heat of battle – putting on 'Saul's armour' could be a big mistake. David would have been hampered by something he did not know how to handle and would not have been able to run at Goliath as he did. Use what has been tested and is real to you.

'Binding and loosing'

There are many prayer phrases around today and 'binding and loosing' is one of the most often used. There is probably not much wrong with it, but let's not simply pick up these words and bandy them around without knowing what they mean. The only thing that sets free is truth, reality. If what we say is not based on truth or reality in our lives then it has no power. We must pray strong prayers to see these people set free but our prayers must be based on reality. It is vital that we are real ourselves and do not do anything simply because someone else does it. When using any method in prayer, we need to ask, 'Is it scriptural?' If the answer is no, then do not hesitate to discard it. If the answer is yes, then we need to ask, 'Is it right for me?' Only if it is real to me should I begin to use it.

The teaching of binding and loosing is usually taken from two places in Scripture. First, in Matthew 16:9, where Jesus is telling Peter the authority that the church has in him. The original version of the *New American Standard Bible* translated this in what appears to be the most accurate way: 'I will give you the keys of the kingdom of heaven; and whatever you shall bind on earth *shall have been* bound in heaven, and whatever you shall loose on earth *shall have been* loosed in heaven.'

The emphasised words are not in later editions but seem to hold the key to the understanding of this verse. Is Jesus saying that whatever the church on earth decides to bind or loose then heaven will follow suit? This would put heaven and the Lord of heaven at the mercy of his people. Surely what it is saying is that first the will of heaven is revealed on a matter concerning what shall be bound and what loosed. At this point the church then agrees with heaven and the matter is ratified. In other words, heaven moves first and then earth responds. It is interesting that Matthew uses these same words in chapter 18:18 about forgiveness and discipline within the church. I would not say that we cannot use these words in any other way but that is the way they are applied here.

The other passage we need to mention is Mark 3:27. There is no way that we can plunder the property of Satan without Satan being bound. These are not just flippant words. The meaning of binding is 'to put under the obligation of the law'. In other words, there is a law at work that has to be obeyed even by Satan. What law can that be? The law that says that Jesus has already bound the strong man. He did it once and for all at Calvary and we read in Ephesians 4:8 that he led captive a host of captives. We can declare today that Satan must release the captives because of what Jesus did two thousand years ago, not because we declare something today. This is the strong foundation that we can pray from; this is how we can plunder the goods. Learn how to pray strongly with others and to declare God's power to break Satan's hold because of the finished work of Jesus on the cross. Do not just mouth words but see the reality behind them. The fellowship I was brought up in used to call it 'executive' prayer. It was the signature at the bottom that ensured the document was carried out. Jesus has finished the work but he wants us to declare this in specific situations with specific people.

Prayer with fasting

Mark 9:14-29 relates how the Lord, after descending from the Mount of Transfiguration, was faced with a demonised boy. Try as they might the disciples could not help the lad and in the end (9:29) Jesus says that this sort will not come out except by prayer and fasting. This, at first sight, might appear to mean that the more we pray and fast the more demons we will see come out. However, I do not believe that this is the meaning of these verses. Here, the demon came out by the command of the Lord and I do not know of any person delivered simply because someone prayed and fasted. What I believe is that the prayer and fasting deepens and broadens our relationship with the Lord so we are ready to face such challenges. The more we know the Lord the more we are prepared to deal with these situations. Again the prayer and fasting go on before the ministry takes place. This is the preparation ground that gives the Lord the insight and ability to deal with the demonised boy.

What we have seen then is that prayer is a vital preparation. A preparation both for us and for those to whom we minister. There is no substitute and prayer must be the key to a successful ministry in God's eyes.

Prayer for deliverance

So far we have talked about the prayer that has gone on beforehand to prepare the way. Prayer for deliverance takes place with the person present. The cultists will have come to realise their need and will be willing to renounce their old way of life and receive Christ. This will not automatically mean that several demons have to be cast out of them. We should not try to bind the spirit of this or that just on the assumption that it must be there. In my experience there has not been the need to cast out spirits from many of those who have been in the cults, although usually some form of deliverance has been needed. In some cases though there will be need for specific deliverance, for instance, some Mormons who have been involved with temple ceremonies for the dead.

An illustration of this can be seen in the gospels. The woman taken in adultery (John 8) had no demons cast out of her. She receive the word of God that could be applied to her life and cause the necessary change – repentance and an acceptance of that word into her life. However, we read of Mary Magdalene that she had seven demons cast out of her. We need to be aware of both possibilities as we help people in prayer and counselling.

Unfortunately there is no A-Z of deliverance, but there are some main areas that we will probably need to cover. Firstly, we will talk about someone who does not need anything cast out of them.

A person has come to the realisation that the group they have been involved with is wrong and they need to confess this. They will *not* need to confess that the people are wrong, and they may still regard them as their friends. Their confession will be that they have been deceived into error and they want to own up to it now. Secondly, they will need to repent and turn their back on the teachings of the group. Testimony should be made that they want to be set free and that no longer will they associate with the beliefs and ethos of the group; they need to renounce the system they were involved in. James 4:4 tells us that if we are friends of these things not of God, we are God's enemy.

Once this has been done, I believe that we can then pray for any influence that there has been over the person's life to be broken in the name of the Lord. The captive can be set free because of the finished work of Jesus Christ. It might help the person you are praying with if they see that the blood and sacrifice of Jesus Christ are totally sufficient to forgive and deliver them from the past. It might help also to declare these facts aloud through reading scriptures such as Revelation 12:11, Ephesians 1:7, Romans 5:9, and Hebrews 13:12.

There are also scriptures that show that it is important to confess specifically what they have been involved in so that the door can be closed completely. Revelation 2:4, 5 tells us that the

Christians in Ephesus had to 'remember from where they had fallen'. We see this principle in Abraham's life too. After leaving God's will for his life and going down to Egypt, he had to return to the exact place he had left. To return to God's will he needed to realise where he had left it.

These first two steps bring a person from the influence of Satan to the influence of the kingdom of God. They first acknowledge to themselves and then confess to the Lord that they have been wrong. Their attitude shows that their repentance is true and a change can take place. But this is still not the end of the praying – it is just the beginning.

We cannot leave them there because there would be a vacuum in their life. Now we need to pray and ask the Holy Spirit to come and fill every nook and cranny of the area that has been left empty. This is vital. In the Old Testament (Exodus 23:29-30) God said that he would not drive all the enemies out of the promised land at once, because the wild animals would take control. He was going to drive them out little by little and the children of Israel would be able to possess each part. As we drive the enemy out of any part of a person's life, the 'land' must come under the Lord's control.

Praying for those demonised

This cannot be a complete treatise on the subject, but you will probably meet the problem at some stage, and I believe we need to deal with it. Let me say first of all that if you come face to face with a demonised person and you have fear about dealing with it, do not get involved. Find someone else you can pass them on to. Fear is Satan's biggest weapon. We should not allow him to win the victory for ever over it, but we must be realistic. When God was preparing the army for Gideon all those who were afraid were sent home (Judges 7:3). When Jehoshophat faced all the enemies he was afraid (2 Chronicles 20). However, he dealt with it and set himself to seek the Lord. Be honest if there is fear in your life but then seek the Lord whose love casts out fear.

Secondly, we should note carefully the *simplicity* of Jesus dealing with demons in Luke 4:35 and 8:32-33, and elsewhere. It may not be possible for us to be always as simple and efficient but we do not need to over-complicate matters. There is a school of thought around that seems to make deliverance a science that needs a PhD. Demons are categorised into many subsections and each must be dealt with differently. So much to learn and if you do it in the wrong order or in the wrong place, things might get worse. Don't be fooled into thinking that deliverance is only for the brainy. Human intelligence has little if anything to do with it; it is the Spirit who teaches us and leads in this matter.

We may talk about 'oppression' or 'possession' but Scripture shows that it is being affected by Satan. The Greek word found in the four gospels is *damonzomai* which translated means 'demonisation,' ie being affected by Satanic forces. Not everyone we deal with in the cults will be demonised and we need to pray that the Holy Spirit will help us discern the situation.

For instance, Luke 4:28 shows Satan using a temporary foothold; the people were enraged with Jesus, and Satan used that to get them to attack him, but just because someone loses their temper from time to time does not mean that they have a 'spirit of rage'. It may be comforting to put the blame there but it is not true and no amount of 'deliverance' will solve the problem. To deal with temper we need to have a fresh understanding of what it means to be crucified with Christ. I remember seeing a well-known evangelist stomping on cigarette packets and binding the spirits of nicotine. I thought then, and still do think, that such an action is not based on Scripture. Many are hooked physically on nicotine as a drug. It is not the spirit of nicotine that needs to be driven out, rather it is the Lord who needs to come in and help them to exercise their will and deny themselves.

But if we discern true demonisation, then the spirit must be cast out. There are a few occasions in Scripture when the spirit was commanded to leave the person without any co-operation on their part, but in practice, it is normal for there to be some co-operation on the part of the person. Usually this takes the form of repenting and turning their back on the practice that opened the doorway in the first place. I would add that I believe that it is dangerous to seek to perform deliverance without the person being willing to put their life under the Lord's sovereignty. How will anything actually change in the long term? Will not Satan simply return – because the doorway is still open – and so make things worse?

Having come to the point of repentance, the demonic influence can be resisted in the name of the Lord. Once a person has stated that he wants to bring his life under the control of the Lord Jesus we can, as Scripture tells us, resist the devil. Then the doorway needs to be closed that had been open for Satan to come in and out just as he wanted, just as the children of Israel needed to close the door on their wanderings in the wilderness (Joshua 5:2-9). We need to make strong prayer and supplication for the grace and mercy of God to close that door now that repentance has come.

We have simply outlined the principles involved and I do not want to give the impression that it will be easy. There will be battles, but if we know our ground we can stand against the enemy. Take heart from Eleazer (1 Chronicles 11:12-14), one of David's mighty men, who stood firm in a barley field because it belonged to the Lord!

Persistence

Whichever way they have come to this place, it is still just the beginning for the cultists who have been set free. Just as there was the need lay the foundation of basic doctrine, so there is the need to continue to pray for them. Pray that they will grow in God and in the knowledge of him. Pray that they will learn to resist Satan and to stand for truth and reality in Christ. Pray that they will be established in the church and be used in the ministry that God calls them to.

We will end this chapter with the remarkable parable in Luke 18:1-8. Here we read about the widow woman who came every day to the judge, repeatedly saying the same thing. It was a plea from her heart and she did not bother finding different words; she was very specific and very practical in what she said. The Lord shows that if this unrighteous judge in the end gave in, how much more will our God in heaven respond to the cries of his people and bring righteous judgement to them. Let us not grow weary but continue to plead and intercede to the righteous judge to act and set these captives free, captives who have been bound by deception although they had sought for the truth. Will not our righteous judge and heavenly Father hear our cries on their behalf?

9

What Do We Believe?
(1) God and the Bible

Often when I have been describing the belief of a cult, Christians have looked at me fairly blankly, either wondering what is wrong with such a belief or knowing it's wrong, but having no idea how to answer it.

No self-respecting firm would ever send representatives out on the road without first giving them ample training about the company and products they represent. Most of us do not welcome door-to-door salesmen at the best of times, but one who doesn't know what he's talking about will certainly not be tolerated for long.

At election time the speeches we hear do not normally tell us what the candidate's party believes but more what the opposition does not. You even wonder if they spend more time looking at the manifesto of the opposition than their own.

These examples can teach us lessons in the Christian life. First, we need to know about the 'company' and 'product' we represent. There is no way we can help others if we cannot explain what we believe. Secondly, although we may talk about the 'opposition' we must also be able to say what we believe and why our 'party' is best. Apologetics are vital when we are speaking with anybody, but even more so with those in the cults, who feel they already have the truth. The word apologetics is derived from the Greek word *apologia* and means 'a reasoned argument' *not* to apologise. The word is used eight times in the New Testament; (Acts 22:1; 25:16; 1 Corinthians 9:3; 2 Corinthians 7:11; Philippians 1:7, 16; 2 Timothy 4:16; 1 Peter 3:15). It means 'a verbal defence, of what one has done or a truth in which one believes'. Again, the word 'defence' is not negative, but a very positive vindication as the scriptures above show. The only way we can do this is to know what we believe and then we can make a clear presentation of the facts.

We are going to look at what the Scriptures teach on several subjects, in order to identify what is false. During our investigation we will also show how we can express to a cult member why we believe the Bible teaches what we claim it does.

God

The Bible never seeks to 'prove' God. Its opening words are that in the beginning God was there. The psalmist says that it is only the fool who says there is no God. Paul in Romans 1:19-20 shows that the evidence of God is all around us. His invisible attributes, eternal power and divine nature are clearly to be seen and there is therefore no excuse for not believing that he exists.

The God of Scripture is infinite. In the beginning he was already there, the only one to be truly eternal. We often think eternal means to have no end but in reality it means to have no beginning or end. God alone fits this description.

God is immutable; that is, he never changes. Hebrews 6:17-18 shows how we can totally rely on God because of his unchanging covenant.

Other attributes the Scriptures give to God are omnipresence – being everywhere (Psalm 139:7-10); omnipotence – he is all-powerful. He spoke and the worlds came into being; he laughs at all that human beings can do (Psalm 2); he alone can stop human beings from doing what they plan to do (Genesis 11:6-9); he is omniscient, – the only one who has perfect knowledge.

Although this great God is the sovereign ruler of the universe, he still reveals himself in a personal way. The 'I AM' (not the 'I was' or 'I will be') always reveals himself to his people not as an impersonal force but as a loving Creator God (Hebrews 1:1-3). He is a loving God who wants all of us to be saved and have an eternal future with him.

So we can clearly see the difference between the God of the Bible and the impersonal force of the New Age and other religions.

Jesus Christ

Most cults will accept God; but most will attack the person and deity of Christ. They will either seek to downgrade Jesus to being something less than God, or they will lift man up to his level. What does Scripture teach?

Is Jesus a created being?

Different groups will twist various scriptures to 'prove' that he is. We will look at one or two of these and see what they really teach.

Often the word *firstborn* is taken to mean 'first to be created'. Let's look for example at Colossians 1:15: 'He is the image of the invisible God, the firstborn over all creation.' The word translated 'firstborn' is the Greek word *prototokos* and means the first-begotten. It can never mean the first one to be born. Its meaning is priority to or pre-eminence over; therefore Jesus is the pre-eminent one over *all* creation and not a created being himself.

The problem arises because most translators use the English word 'firstborn' as it best describes the Greek. We need to discover what the Greek word actually means and how it was used at the time the New Testament was written. The word is also used in Colossians 1:18. Does it mean that Jesus was the first one to be born from the dead? That could not be true because in the New Testament there were at least three others before Jesus, including Lazarus, apart from those mentioned in the Old Testament. Is the scripture wrong? It must be if Jesus is called the first one to be born from the dead. There is no confusion however when we take the true meaning of the Greek word as position, place or ranking. This is clearly seen in the Old Testament where on at least two occasions the first to be born lost the position of 'firstborn' to the second to be born. 'Firstborn' has always, in the Hebrew tradition, had to do with place and pre-eminence. Colossians makes this abundantly clear: '. . . that He might come to have first place in everything' (1:18).

Greek scholar W. E. Vine, in his *Dictionary of New Testament Words*, points out that in Exodus 4:22 it was impossible for the whole of Israel to be the firstborn. It must be referring to their position and place before the Lord. Again in Deuteronomy 21:16-17 a second born son can become the firstborn by giving him the pre-eminence! We could also refer to Jeremiah 31:9 'Ephraim is my firstborn'. God has told a lie, because Ephraim was not the first to be born! The explanation is found in Genesis 48 where Israel blessed Ephraim and gave him the pre-eminence although he was not first to be born.

Did Christ have a pre-existence?

There are groups who say that Christ did not exist until he came to earth. However John 1:1-5 is clearly talking about a person who is the Christ and who was with God in the beginning. Through him all things came into being, and life was in him. This cannot speak of an inanimate object but must speak of the *person* of Christ.

Philippians 2:6-7 shows that just as Jesus actually existed as man, he had already existed as God. Finally we can also mention John 8:58 that succinctly says that 'before Abraham was, I AM'. Jesus was in existence before Abraham and therefore clearly had a life before he came to earth.

What was declared at his birth?

Many cults teach that Jesus did not really become the Christ until his baptism, but the angel's message was quite clear: '. . . for *today* in the city of David there has been born for you a Saviour, *who is* Christ the Lord (Luke 2:11, my italics).

Who does the Bible declare that Jesus is?

In John 5:16 we find Jesus being persecuted for healing on the Sabbath. His response to this begins: 'My Father . . .'. From this the Jews understood that Jesus was claiming to be equal with God.

This may seem straightforward and easily understood, but still some groups will still try to wriggle round the scripture. They will use arguments such as that it was the unbelieving Jews who were calling Jesus God and we should not believe what unbelieving Jews say! The answer to this argument comes in two stages.

First, Jesus had a way of saying the most profound things so that no one could understand him (eg the parable of the sower in Matthew 13). But here he spoke plainly so that the people understood. Secondly, Jesus was a Jew and understood how the Jewish mind worked. He knew that when he said, 'My Father . . .' the Jews would understand that he was claiming to be of the same substance as Jehovah, ie God.

If Jesus is *not* equal with God who has got it wrong – Jesus, or the Jews who believed what Jesus was saying? Of course in these circumstances Jesus would be at fault. This would make him a liar and a fraud. He obviously is neither of these things and therefore the statement that he was claiming to be equal with God must be correct.

John 20:24-30 records the second time that Jesus appeared to the disciples, and the first time that Thomas sees him. Thomas's response was to acknowledge Jesus as 'my Lord and my *God*.' Again this would seem fairly clear, but some groups will argue that it does not really mean what it says. Read the verse carefully. First it clearly says that Thomas was speaking to Jesus. Secondly, the Greek here is emphatic; Thomas' words are *ho theos*, the God – not just *a* god. If this were not so Jesus would have had to rebuke Thomas, but in verse 29 he commends all those who will believe the same as Thomas believed. In the midst of those who were to go out to teach the early church, Jesus accepts the acclamation that he was God. What did the apostles believe? They believed that Jesus was God. What must we believe from this incident? Clearly that Jesus knowingly and readily accepted the acclamation of being God.

In Revelation 5:13-14 we have an insight into Jesus' heavenly ministry. Who is receiving this honour, glory and worship? The One on the throne (The Father) *and* the Lamb (Jesus). Are we not to do what heaven is doing?

Point out that *every creature* gives this to Jesus, who therefore *cannot* be a created being. If Jesus is less than God, if he is really a created being, even a created heavenly being, the Bible would show that there was idol worship in heaven – creature worshipping creature. No angels, except fallen ones, no other heavenly creatures ever receive worship; only God receives worship in his heavenly kingdom. Jesus therefore must be God.

The Holy Spirit

In the fourth century there was a group known as the Pneumatomachians, literally, 'fighters against the Spirit'. Their attack was against the deity of the Holy Spirit. There are many cult groups today who continue this fight. Some will even take it further and deny not only his deity but his personality too. They will claim that he is not at work in this age and the gifts of the Holy Spirit must be satanically inspired.

In talking about the Holy Spirit to such groups we need to cover three areas:

1.   Does the Bible show the Holy Spirit to be God?
2.   Does the Bible show that the Holy Spirit has a personality?
3.   What does the Bible have to say concerning the work of the Holy Spirit among Christians today?

We need to remember that this will not be just an intellectual battle, and we will not be just showing off our biblical knowledge; we will be using scripture in such a way as to give the Holy Spirit himself an opportunity to reveal the truth. 'A natural man does not accept the things of the Spirit of God; for they are foolishness to him, and he cannot understand them, because they are spiritually appraised' (1 Corinthians 2:14).

Does the Bible show the Holy Spirit to be God?

An unbiased reading of Scripture will show several references that prove beyond any reasonable doubt that the Holy Spirit is God. First let's look at what Jesus said of the Holy Spirit: 'And I will ask the Father, and He will give you another Helper, that he may be with you for ever' (John 14:16).

W. E. Vine in his *Greek Expository Dictionary* points out that the Greek word for 'another' in John 14:16, 'denotes another *of the same kind*'. This one who was coming would be of the same kind as Jesus – not different. Just as Jesus was of the 'substance' of God, the Holy Spirit would be of the same kind.

The Bible reveals that the Holy Spirit is distinct from the Father and the Son (John 14:16 and Acts 2:33), but it also gives a simple and clear declaration that the Holy Spirit is God. In Acts 5:3 we find that Ananias is said to have lied to the Holy

Spirit, but in the very next verse Peter says that Ananias lied to God. To Peter and all in the early church, the Holy Spirit *was* God.

The Holy Spirit in the New Testament is identified with the Yahweh (Jehovah) of the Old Testament. See for example Hebrews 3:7-11 where the Holy Spirit tells us that *he* was provoked and tested. As a result he said, 'They shall not enter my rest'. This passage in Hebrews is quoting from Psalm 95:7-11, and if you refer back to those verses you will find the Psalmist is speaking of God. And further back still, where the incident is originally recorded in Numbers 14:23-30, we see that it is the 'Lord Jehovah' who is speaking. The Holy Spirit is called by this name reserved for God. Scripture is not out to confuse us, and if it interchanges the Holy Spirit and God it is to show us that the Holy Spirit *is* God.

Divine works that God alone can accomplish are shown to be the work of the Holy Spirit. For instance, the work of creation is attributed to the Holy Spirit in Job 33:4 and Psalm 104:25-30, and Isaiah 44:24 and 45:18 show this is solely God's work. Also resurrection (Romans 8:11); regeneration (John 3:5-6 and Titus 3:5) and the very important work of sanctification (Romans 15:16; 1 Corinthians 6:11; 2 Thessalonians 2:13 and 1 Peter 1:1-2).

Scripture gives further evidence of the deity of the Holy Spirit by showing he has attributes only found within God. He is eternal (Hebrews 9:14); omnipresent (Psalm 139:7-10); omnipotent (Luke 1:35; Romans 15:13-19 and 1 Corinthians 12:7-11); and omniscient (1 Corinthians 2:10-11 and Isaiah 40:13-14).

Note too the way that Scripture puts the name of the Holy Spirit along with the name of the Father and the name of the Son. Two examples of this are found in the apostolic commission (Matthew 28:19-20) and the benediction in 2 Corinthians 13:14.

A further significant piece of evidence is that the apostles recognised the sovereignty or lordship of the Spirit. Paul writes:

> But whenever a man turns to the Lord, the veil is taken away. Now the Lord is the Spirit; and where the Spirit of the Lord is, there is liberty. But we all, with unveiled face beholding as in a mirror the glory of the Lord, are being transformed into the same image from glory to glory, just as from the Lord, the Spirit (2 Corinthians 3:16-18).

We will add one final point here by quoting from E. H. Bancroft:

> The Holy Spirit can be blasphemed, and this is possible only of God. As spirit is nothing less than the innermost principle of life, and the spirit of man is man himself, so the Spirit of God must be God Himself (1 Cor 2:11). Thus the Scriptures teach that the Holy Spirit is a person having all the divine attributes and able to do all divine works (E. H. Bancroft, *Christian Theology*, p. 160).

Does the Bible show that the Holy Spirit has a personality?

Clearly the Bible shows that the Holy Spirit is a *power* (see for instance, Luke 1:35), but I believe it also gives conclusive evidence of his *personality*.

Jesus Christ is called the *Advocate* in 1 John 2:1. The same Greek word translated *Comforter*, is used of the Holy Spirit in John 14:16. An impersonal force could not fulfil the function described here. The Holy Spirit is to be the *Paraclete*, meaning someone who goes to court to speak for you – not a job for an impersonal force!

Another indication that the Scripture gives of the personality of the Holy Spirit is found in John 16:7-15. Here Jesus uses the masculine 'he' of the Holy Spirit twelve times although the noun translated 'spirit' is neuter. If these verses were to be grammatically correct they would have been written with the Holy Spirit being called 'it'. The fact that 'he' is used is a deliberate indication of the personality of the Holy Spirit.

> But I tell you the truth, it is to your advantage that I go away; for if I do not go away, the Helper shall not come to you; but if go, I will send *Him* to you. And *He*, when *He* comes, will convict the world concerning sin, and righteousness, and judgement . . . But when *He* the Spirit of truth, comes, *He* will guide you into all truth; for *He* will not speak on *His* own initiative, but whatever *He* hears, *He* will speak; and *He* will disclose to you what is to come. *He* shall glorify Me; for *He* shall take of Mine, and shall disclose it to you. All things that the Father has are Mine; therefore I said, that *He* takes of Mine and will disclose it to you (John 16:7-8, 13-15, italics added).

Personality is not just dependent on outward form and actions but on the life within. There are three areas that need to be present for someone to be classed as a person: intellect, will, and emotion.

First, let us look at what the Scriptures show concerning the Holy Spirit and an intellect. John 14:26 tells us that the Holy Spirit can teach and this is a sign of intellect. Romans 8:26-27 shows us that the Holy Spirit intercedes for us. Again a sign of intellect. Greek scholar W. E. Vine's definition of 'intercession' shows that an impersonal force could not do it:

> Primarily to fall in with, meet with in order to converse; then to make petition, especially to make intercession, plead with a person, either for or against others (W. E. Vine, *Dictionary of New Testament Words*, Vol. 2, p. 267).

1 Corinthians 2:10-11 also tells us that the Holy Spirit can know the thoughts of God. A third clear sign that the Holy Spirit has an intellect.

Secondly what do the Scriptures show concerning the Holy Spirit and a will?

Acts 8:29, 39 among other Scriptures, (see also Acts 10:19-20 and 16:6-7) show the Holy Spirit's work in directing the early church. Here he directs Philip in his ministry, a clear sign that the Holy Spirit has a will.

1 Corinthians 12:11 is clear that the Holy Spirit has a will of his own and can make decisions. He distributes the gifts just as he *wills*. W. E. Vine tells us the Greek word used here means, 'to wish, to will deliberately . . . the deliberate exercise of the will'. (*Dictionary of New Testament Words*, Vol. 1, p. 299). Again we must conclude beyond all reasonable doubt that the Holy Spirit has a will.

Thirdly and finally, we need to see what the Scriptures show concerning the Holy Spirit and emotions.

We see that the Holy Spirit can love, Romans 15:30 and can comfort, Acts 9:31, both attributes that come from the heart and show emotion.

Ephesians 4:30 says that the Holy Spirit can be grieved. We again turn to W. E. Vine for the meaning of the Greek word used. It 'denotes to cause pain, or grief, to distress, grieve'. (Vine's *Dictionary of New Testament Words*, Vol. 2, p. 178).

According to the Bible, the Holy Spirit possesses an intellect, a will and emotions and can therefore be shown to be a person.

What does the Bible have to say concerning the work of the Holy Spirit among Christians today?

We already touched upon this in Chapter 7 when we were looking at the work of the Holy Spirit for today. Most will accept that 'holy spirit' as an impersonal force can be an extension of the power of God and can help us to one degree or another. Many will also accept that the fruit of the Spirit is necessary for our lives today. Can we then divorce this work of the Holy Spirit from his gifts which he distributes as he wills?

Some cults will say that the gifts of the Holy Spirit are not for today. They were only necessary to see the early church established or until that which is perfect – the Bible – came into being. This last thought comes from 1 Corinthians 13:10 that says that when that which is perfect comes the gifts that are partial will cease. However, what is 'that which is perfect', and has it come? As great as the Bible is, I do not believe it is 'that which is perfect'. There is still a greater revelation for us when God sets up his kingdom and that which the Bible points forward to will be a reality. When we see the Lord face to face we will not need the gifts, but until then they reveal God to people and we should be seeking him to release them through us for the ministry to the cults among other things.

The work of the Holy Spirit in giving gifts is vital to bring in fullness and completeness, and I do not believe we can divorce this aspect of his work from others that Scripture shows he is doing. Let us then summarise the way the Bible shows that the Holy Spirit is working in the church today.

The church came into being via the Holy Spirit (Acts 2:1-4), and he alone is the One who can bring unity (1 Corinthians 12:12-27 and Ephesians 4:1-6).

He is the One who confers gifts and graces upon God's children to fulfil the work of the Lord (Romans 12:6-8, 1 Corinthians 12:4-11, Galatians 5:22-26, and Ephesians 4:8-13).

The Holy Spirit is the One who teaches Christians and the One who directs the church in its outreach to the world (John 14:26, 1 John 2:20, 27, Acts 13:1-3, 16:7 and 20:28).

All aspects of the life of the church – preaching, prayer, etc – are dependent on the work of the Holy Spirit (Acts 10:44, 1 Corinthians 2:1-5, Romans 8:26-27, and Ephesians 5:18-19).

If the third person of the Trinity, the Holy Spirit, ceased his work on earth today there would be no Christian work. Sadly, the cults are not moving under the Holy Spirit and that is why they are not fulfilling a Christian ministry and do not even want to admit his work exists.

Lovingly we need to present to them the necessity for knowing the work of the Holy Spirit today, and to show that he needs to be at work in their own lives and in the life of the group to which they belong.

The Trinity

Never try to prove the existence of the Trinity purely from a logical point of view. It is impossible. The Trinity is not logical to the human mind. We believe the Trinity with our hearts. We can explain that the chemical formula H_2O can be found as ice, water or steam. That certainly shows the idea behind the Trinity but it does not prove the Trinity exists. What we need to be able to show to the religious cults who spend their life denying the existence of the Trinity, is that the Bible reveals it. Whether we can accept it logically is irrelevant if the revelation of the word of God is plain for us to see.

To most cult groups the Trinity is a problem and when the subject comes up many appear to lose interest. To groups such as the Jehovah's Witnesses, if you mention the word you are seen as part of the apostate church. They will make much of the fact that it is a pagan doctrine. They have even produced a colour booklet, *Should You Believe in the Trinity?* which clearly shows that they are right! They delight in giving this to church-goers to confuse them.

Should we avoid the subject then? Not if we understand our own doctrine of the Trinity. Without understanding these things ourselves, there is little hope of expressing these truths to the sceptical in a convincing way.

What follows is not a full treatise on the Trinity; there are other books that have undertaken that. What I want to do is to

show that the Scriptures answer the main arguments put
forward by the cults.

The Trinity is beyond reason

The religious cults that we are speaking to will all believe in
God and the revelation of him as they see it in the Bible. But
God himself is beyond human reason. Speaking to bring the
world into being is not something we can reason out. The fact
that God is everywhere, always, and can listen and speak to
everyone is beyond reason. If therefore God is beyond human
reason it is not surprising that doctrines concerning God also
defy reason. We do not, and indeed cannot fully comprehend
God with our minds; we need to use our spirits too. Certainly
the Trinity is beyond reason, but it is not beyond revelation. Just
as we do not reject God because we cannot reason him out, we
should not reject the Trinity because it is beyond our mental
capacity to understand it.

Further study can be undertaken with such scriptures as
Isaiah 55:11, John 1:14, 16:13-15, 1 Corinthians 2:9, 10, 14 and
2 Corinthians 3:5-18.

The sum of all its parts

Good defence lawyers will always seek to fragment the evidence brought against their client. They will try to isolate
certain aspects of the testimony and show the weakness of it.
The prosecution will seek to show that the strength of their case
is that all the parts fit together and lead to one conclusion
beyond any reasonable doubt.

Jehovah's Witnesses, among other cult members, delight in
telling people that the word 'Trinity' is not found in the Bible.
That is correct, but the word was only coined to describe certain
aspects of the Godhead and their relationship to each other.
There are even some clues to the Trinity in the Old Testament.
Deuteronomy 6:4 tells us that there is One true God, with 'One'

being a composite not singular. There are also clues showing that God is more than one person. See for instance Isaiah 48:16 and 63:9-10. However, if the Old Testament has the doctrine in shadow form, the New Testament clearly defines what we mean by the word 'Trinity'.

There are three distinct persons. Scriptures such as Matthew 28:19 and 1 Corinthians 12:4-6 describe the three. We can also see from John 5:37 that Jesus distinguishes himself from the Father. Then in John 14:16, the Holy Spirit is called 'another', distinguishing him from both Father and Son.

The Father is God. This is not usually disputed and we have already looked at this aspect.

Jesus is God. Again we have already dealt with this and verses such as John 5:21, 20:28 and Hebrews 1:3 clearly show it to be true.

The Holy Spirit is God. Many verses including Acts 5:3-4 and 2 Corinthians 3:16-18 show the truth of this statement.

All these specific aspects of the Trinity are clearly shown to be true according to the word of God. The word 'Trinity' may not appear in the Bible but the Bible clearly teaches the idea of the Trinity in all its aspects.

The Bible

Can we rely on the Bible? We would answer a resounding 'yes!'. Can we then rely on the Bible more than any other 'religious' book? Again we would answer 'yes' and would present the following evidence. The *Koran*, *The Book of Mormon*, or *Science and Health with Key to the Scriptures* cannot pass all the following tests as well as the Bible can. They may pass one or two but not all.

The composition

No other book has been written by such a variety of human authors, living in such separated parts of the world over a time span of hundreds of years. Not only do we have the human impossibility of getting all the writings together, but when they are brought into one place, they miraculously fit to a divine pattern. The composition of the Bible clearly shows the hand of an eternal God, not the work of a human committee.

The content

Nothing proves the Bible more than the test of time. The Bible talks about 'the circle of the earth' when everyone in those days thought the world was flat. Abraham was told about the millions of stars when comparatively few were visible. The Bible talked about 'this great city of Babylon' when it did not seem even to exist. Astronomy, archaeology, cosmology, geology and other sciences have all clearly proved statements in the Bible instead of showing them to be lies.

The prophecy

At least 700 years before it happened, the Bible foretold where Jesus would be born, how he would be born, why he would be born, and what would happen to him through his life. No one could have made that up. And it needed the intervention of an eternal God to bring it all to pass.

The experience

No book has the power to change lives as the Bible does with its message of Calvary and Pentecost. Many other 'religious' books have passed away, but the Lord has watched over his word. He has said that heaven and earth – and therefore all other books – will pass away before the Bible does.

The Bible can be trusted totally and relied upon completely. Scripture, as the word of God, is 'breathed out' and inspired by the Holy Spirit. The men who penned the words were not perfect – the Bible makes that abundantly clear – but the words inspired by the Holy Spirit are perfect. They are there to make us complete, equipped for everything and lacking nothing (2 Timothy 3:17).

10

What Do We Believe?
(2) Salvation

God makes it clear that there is nothing that we can do to deserve God's salvation or to earn it. The moment we try to walk along the path of works, we are outside God's revelation. However, we do need to co-operate with God and accept what he has done, in order to receive salvation. Salvation is a finished work; nothing can be added to it. When Jesus said, 'It is finished', he meant it. Humanity had become separated from God and the only way back was by blood sacrifice. The continual sacrifice of bulls and goats could only be temporary. The Book of Hebrews shows us that the permanent solution was the sacrifice, once and for all, by Jesus Christ.

From our side, how do we need to co-operate with God to receive salvation? There must be repentance, the voluntary change of mind of a sinner turning away from sin, an act of the will. We do not have the power to change our lives, but by applying our will to turn away from the past we show God our desire to receive salvation. Repentance, as it were, empties out the old and makes room for the new to be received. As John 1:12 says, 'As many as received Him to them He gave the right to become children of God'. We need then positively to receive Christ into our lives to fulfil his work in us. Salvation has nothing to do with us; it is the gift of God that must be received by faith based on what God has said (Ephesians 2:8-10). There are no works that we can do to receive salvation. We will be looking at this in more detail later in this chapter.

At this point we are justified. It is vitally important that we understand what that means, otherwise we will be grovelling around in the mire instead of standing on the rock. Justification means that God has declared us righteous and treats us as such. It has nothing to do with what we are as individuals, nor what we have accomplished; it is an act of declaration by God. Our place is to realise what God has done and live in the good of it. You could never in a thousand lifetimes, never in a million hours of prayer bring yourself to righteousness. But God has pronounced it and he treats us as righteous. That is the place we start from.

The prodigal son is a great example of justification. Returning from the pigsty and from wasting his inheritance he found himself clothed immediately with the robe of righteousness (Luke 15:22). However, you would not expect the son to stay as he was underneath, full of dirt and grime. You would expect ongoing changes that would show his responsibility in the house. For a start you would expect him to have a bath! And that is the process of sanctification. Justification is a once and for all act as Romans 5:1 shows, 'having been justified'. Sanctification is an ongoing process, '. . . resulting in sanctification' (Romans 6:19). We are being continually changed into his likeness.

Salvation by works or Faith?

Most cults that you will meet have the view that works, to one degree or another, are vital to salvation. We want to empha- sise the word *vital* because we believe that works do have their place and Christians should not just be pew-warmers and sermon-fodder. Can we, however, be saved without the use of works? Is it possible to come into a true relationship with Jesus Christ and know the forgiveness of sins without doing certain works?

Many groups will have quite complicated arguments and a well developed 'theology' to show their belief from Scripture. Simply put, though, what they are saying is that there is no way that we can be saved without some action on our part. Just responding to what Jesus said and receiving the benefits of what he has already accomplished is not enough.

The type of work needing to be accomplished will be slightly different depending on the group you are dealing with. Some groups will claim that you must join their group to be saved, even going as far as to say that there is no salvation outside their group. You certainly need Jesus but you also need to make a human commitment to an earthly group and work with them. Leave the confines of the group and you will leave your salvation behind.

There will be others who will claim that salvation can only come when the individual has accurate knowledge. The Watchtower Society has even translated the word 'know' in John 17:3 to prove this: eternal life is equated to 'taking in accurate knowlege'. Our mental capacity becomes essential to being saved. This of course will immediately give the intelligent an unfair advantage and may mean that some can never be saved because of their lack of understanding. Is our God unfair and partial to rule out some people from salvation?

Still others will say that you must believe in the writings of a particular person who alone can lead you to the clear truth of salvation. Doing what they say is vital to salvation and those who do not follow them will never be saved.

Whatever slight variations there may be, the Scriptures show a different picture. We will look together at the teaching of the Bible on faith and works and see what the relationship is. We must know what is essential for our salvation and what place works have in our relationship with God. If we are not clear on this we will never be able to help those who are striving through works to reach God.

Should I rely on a person?

There are many within the cults who have been told that they must put all their trust in one person as this act alone will lead them to salvation. We have already looked at the subject of authoritarianism in Chapter 3 but we shall look at a couple of Scriptures here.

First we are taught that we are never to put our trust solely in a created man or woman, no matter how great he or she is. The Psalmist declared, 'It is better to take refuge in the Lord than trust in man. It is better to take refuge in the Lord than to trust in princes' (Psalm 118:8-9). Faith is to be placed in God alone (Mark 11:22). He alone cannot be moved.

Of course God has given us our brothers and sisters for strength and help but not to rely on them instead of relying on God. True leadership will always point us to rely on the Lord and not encourage us to be dependent on another human being. If a man or woman becomes the centre of our faith and trust there is something very wrong.

Another thing that we need to be clear about is that nowhere in the New Testament do we see someone working for an organisation to find God. Today, there are groups who give the impression that when you leave them you leave behind your salvation. What causes someone to be saved? The work of the Holy Spirit within the life. Can then the outward act of leaving a particular group cause me to lose my salvation? Such a teaching has no foundation in logic let alone in Scripture. Some group members will need help to understand exactly what they do believe because their leaders may have confused them into accepting two opposites – salvation by faith and by works! A conversation to help them see the truth could go something like this;

> CHRISTIAN: Would you say that you are saved by faith or by works?
>
> CULT MEMBER: Definitely by faith.
>
> CHRISTIAN: You believe then that your salvation is based on a relationship with Jesus Christ alone?
>
> CULT MEMBER: Yes.
>
> CHRISTIAN: Just suppose that you left your group tomorrow and unfortunately died the week after. Is your salvation secure?
>
> CULT MEMBER: No, we can never be presumptuous; we have to stay loyal to God's people here on earth.
>
> CHRISTIAN: But only your outward state has changed. You still have the same faith within.
>
> CULT MEMBER: That does not matter, I would have left the group that God is using.
>
> CHRISTIAN: Then your faith is in the outward belonging to the group and not the inward relationship with God.
>
> CULT MEMBER: Well . . .

Faith is not of human origin

While talking to a cult member, it will probably not be necessary to give a full theological explanation of faith. It will certainly help, though, if you point out one or two things. The first statement you could make is that faith is not of human origin. This means that when I say that I am saved by faith it cannot mean that I am saved by works; the two are opposites.

Romans 10:17 shows that faith comes from receiving the word of Christ. Naturally we do not have faith to tell a mountain to go into the sea (Matthew 17:20). Any natural 'faith' we have could not survive the testing by fire mentioned in 1 Peter 1:7. True faith that we have comes from God, is increased by God and is tested by God. It is not positive thinking, mind over matter, or anything else that we try to do.

Faith is also shown to be interlinked with our relationship with the Lord, not an organisation. Galatians 2:20 reveals that Paul lived his new life by God's faith. How did he come to that place? Through knowing the reality of what it meant to be crucified with Christ. At that point he no longer lived by his own strength and motivation; now it was Christ's. Faith in Paul's life was clearly because of a relationship with Jesus Christ not the organisation that he had been involved in before.

Luke 17:5 records the request of the apostles to increase their faith and the Lord's answer is very revealing. He tells the parable of the servant working all day in the field and then still having to come in and prepare his master's food etc. The slave will not receive any special commendation because that is his relationship with the master. How did the Lord tell them to increase their faith? Should they join a particular group? Should they listen to the teaching of a particular man? No, they should ensure that their relationship with their Master is right. They should ensure that they are being obedient to all that he has said and then their faith will be increased.

Opportunity missed

The story of Mary and Martha recorded in Luke 10:38-42 is an excellent example of works in the New Testament. Jesus was invited into the home of Mary and Martha. Mary took the opportunity to sit at the Lord's feet and listen to his words. Martha on the other hand was flapping around doing many things, most of which were probably legitimate. However, whether the works were good or bad is not the point; they did not bring her closer to the Lord. On that day Martha should have dropped her works and taken the opportunity to receive the Lord and his word.

The end of the story and the effect it had can be found in John 6:28-29. In the crowded room all the spectators were receiving from Jesus but few gave thought as to his needs. It was Mary who was then ready to give to the Lord. She knew in her spirit what he needed and was prepared to do the work. She had been prepared and received faith from sitting at the Lord's feet and now she could get involved with the works. We will see in a moment other Scriptures that show that this is the correct order.

Does eternal life come from working?

We need to ask this question because some groups will specifically say that they can work for the reward of eternal life. It is simply saying that works are essential for salvation in a different way. However, there are some clear Scriptural passages that we can look at that show it is impossible to receive eternal life as wages for our works.

Luke 10:25-28 and 18:18-23 record very similar stories. In both cases the question was asked, 'What can I do to inherit eternal life?' Jesus answers both enquirers in a similar way. The lawyer in Luke 10 immediately tells Jesus what is written in the law: 'You shall love the Lord your God . . .'. You are correct, replies Jesus, go and do that and you will have eternal life. Do what? Ensure that your relationship is right with the Lord. Eternal life is not a reward for doing anything; it is given freely to those who place a relationship with God at the centre of their lives.

The rich young ruler in Luke 18 comes to the same place via a slightly different route. Jesus tells him all the commandments of how to act towards men – in other words what works he should be manifesting. I've done all that, replies the ruler. Interestingly Jesus does not deny this but simply adds one other thing that he has not done. Now he needs to put aside the possessions that were in the centre of his life to ensure that God was at the centre. Again, eternal life does not come from doing works on earth but having a right relationship with God in heaven.

We mentioned earlier those who feel knowledge is important for salvation. John 5:39 shows beyond any question that eternal life cannot come from taking in knowledge – it comes from Jesus.

Why then does the Bible mention works?

This is a very fair question because if we should not be doing works why does the Bible confuse us by mentioning them? We need to be clear, it is not that we should not be doing works but that we must get them in their right place. There is no way we can be saved and receive eternal life by works but once saved there are works for us to do.

Philippians 2:12 is very helpful here, reminding us that we are to *work out* our salvation, not work towards it.

Whenever you talk about works and faith with a cult member, it is almost inevitable that they will mention James 2:22. It is necessary therefore that we understand what is being said here. James begins the chapter by saying, 'My brethren, do not hold your faith . . .' So it becomes apparent immediately that he was writing to 'the brethren', those who had already received Christ and already had faith. What he goes on to show is that to have faith that is not expressed by works is useless.

Faith necessarily leads to good works . . . faith which does not lead men to act upon commands and promises of Christ – or, in other words, does not lead to obedience, is called in Scripture a 'dead,' that is, an unreal faith. E. H. Bancroft, *Christian Theology*, p. 253.

James 2:22 shows that works *perfect* our faith. There is no point in claiming that we have faith if we do not show it. Works express what faith is already; they do not create faith. This whole subject is best summed up in Ephesians 2:8-10:

> For by grace you have been saved through faith; and that not of yourselves, it is the gift of God; not as a result of works, that no one should boast. For we are His workmanship, created in Christ Jesus for good works, which God prepared beforehand, that we should walk in them.

The order is highlighted by these verses. Works can do nothing to enable us to receive salvation. It is God's gift alone and all we can do is get down on our knees and receive gratefully and humbly what he is offering to us. However, once we are saved, there are works prepared for us to do. We are not working *towards* our salvation but working *out* our salvation. This is the biblical picture of works and faith.

Is baptism essential for salvation?

Many cults will say that to be saved you must be baptised. Some will even go as far as to say that unless you are baptised *in our church* you are not saved. Is this what Scripture teaches or is this a clear sign of 'another' gospel? We are not asking if baptism is an important act; there is no doubt in my mind that Scripture commands us to be baptised by immersion as believers, but that is not the subject in question. What we need to answer is, does the Bible show that baptism is *essential* for salvation? In other words is there any way that I can know the saving work of Jesus Christ in my life if I am not baptised?' Alternatively, if as we say baptism is an important act, does it follow salvation? Also does it give a clear testimony to both those on earth and the principalities and powers of what has already happened?

The groups that teach that baptism is essential for salvation will normally use several verses to prove this doctrine from Scripture. These are the ones we need to look at and understand. We can then talk to the cult member and show them that maybe the scriptures they thought proved one thing actually teach another.

There are also some verses in the Bible that give a positive declaration of salvation without baptism and some groups admit that there are problems in explaining them. These, therefore, are often good to use at the beginning to introduce the subject.

Luke 23:42-43 records the repentance of the thief on the cross. He is told that he will be with the Lord that day and yet he never received baptism. Baptism was certainly not essential to the salvation of that man. This also highlights the teaching of Jesus concerning salvation and baptism. He was baptised under John's baptism but he did not teach that if anyone was to be saved they must be baptised. We have clear declarations such as John 3:16, where a clear promise of salvation and deliverance is made providing there is an acting on what the person has heard. No mention is made at all of baptism and yet the word of God says this person will not perish but have everlasting life.

We can see a similar incident in Romans 10:9-10, 13. Here Paul, under the inspiration of the Holy Spirit, says that if we call on the Lord we will be saved. If we confess with our mouth and believe in our heart we shall be saved. This is God's word and cannot be added to or subtracted from and it gives a clear promise of salvation without baptism.

This same situation is found in 1 Corinthians 15:1-5 where Paul makes known the essentials of the gospel. These were the things that were of first importance. In a chapter where he was going to use an illustration of those who baptised for the dead,

I am sure he would have not left out baptism if it was essential. However, the definition is all about the person of Christ and not about baptism. Christ died, he was buried, he rose again and he appeared. This is the gospel, centred in the person and the work of Jesus Christ, not what I can do.

Such a presentation should lay the foundation for talking about verses in Scripture that may appear to show that baptism is essential for salvation.

> And Peter said to them, 'Repent, and let each of you be baptised in the name of Jesus Christ for the forgiveness of your sins; and you shall receive the gift of the Holy Spirit (Acts 2:38).

If this verse is taken out of context it could possibly mean that you need to be baptised to be saved. Initially it does link 'remission of sins' with both repentance and baptism. However, we need to know what the phrase 'for the remission of sins', actually means. Does it mean 'in order to', because then the verse would clearly show that baptism was essential if we want our sins forgiven? The Greek word translated 'for' is *eis* and it is used some 1488 times in the New Testament. In all these hundreds of times it is never translated 'in order to'. Young's *Concise Critical Bible Commentary* renders it literally, 'with a view to a letting go of sins'. If Peter does not mean to say that baptism was essential to be saved, just what was he meaning to say? Peter was talking to Jews in whose mind actions always followed faith. In such a context it would be natural therefore for Peter to talk about the action as well as the faith. However, what is also very instructive is to note that on other occasions, eg Acts 2:21 and 3:19, he did not mention baptism. Does it mean that what Peter said on those occasions was not the true gospel and the people who acted on his words were not saved? That cannot be true but what is seen is that there are times when baptism is mentioned and there are times when it is not. The common factors, which are *always* mentioned, are the repenting and calling on the Lord. These are shown to be the essentials of the gospel.

We must always consider the whole of Scripture and does that mean that John 3:16 and Ephesians 2:8-10 along with the other Scriptures mentioned are only half truths? No, God does not make such mistakes. He ensures that the essential elements of the gospel are always preached.

> Or do you not know that all of us who have been baptized into Christ Jesus have been baptized into His death? Therefore we have been buried with Him through baptism into death, in order that as Christ was raised from the dead through the glory of the Father, so we too might walk in newness of life (Romans 6:3-4).

There are several baptisms mentioned in the Scriptures and each has three elements.

1. The person doing the baptising.
2. The person being baptised.
3. The medium into which they are baptised.

Romans 6 is not talking about a literal baptism into water but being 'baptised into Christ'. These verses are not talking about an outward act that takes place in water but rather an inward act that takes place when you receive Jesus Christ. When you look carefully at these verses you will see that they actually prove that water baptism is *not* essential for salvation. Paul was talking about an inward experience not an outward one that brought these people to new birth and new resurrection life.

> And corresponding to that, baptism now saves you – not the removal of dirt from the flesh, but an appeal to God for a good conscience – through the resurrection of Jesus Christ (1 Peter 3:21).

This Scripture at first glance may appear to say that baptism now saves you, but note in the previous verses what it is corresponding to. Baptism *saving* you corresponds to the flood. We need to discover two things here. What actually saved the people from the flood and what was the salvation from and what was it to.

If this was to teach us that New Testament baptism saves, then we would need to see that it was the water that saved Noah and his family. However, the water did not save them; rather the opposite – it nearly destroyed them. What actually saved them was the ark. We need to discover in New Testament terms what or whom the Old Testament picture of the ark represents, and the answer is not baptism but Jesus Christ. Being put into water does not save us; our safety comes from being in Christ and having a sure relationship with him.

What sort of salvation was this? Are we talking about the salvation of receiving Christ into the life? No, in Old Testament terms, they needed that relationship before they got into the ark. This was a salvation that would take them out of one world system into another. Salvation is not being used here in the sense of being born again. It is a full deliverance, through God's judgement, into the new world order that Christ has yet to set up on earth.

He who has believed and been baptized shall be saved; but he who has disbelieved shall be condemned (Mark 16:16).

Note here that condemnation does not come because of lack of *baptism* but because of not *believing*. There is no evidence from this verse to show that baptism is essential for salvation but it does show that believing is essential. This verse also needs to be compared with Matthew 28:19. Here the disciples – those who had already repented and entered Christ's school – are then baptised.

And now why do you delay? Arise, and be baptized, and wash away your sins, calling on His name (Acts 22:16).

Again this verse seems to say that when Paul was baptised, he washed his sins away. Does this fit in with the evidence that we have concerning Paul's conversion? If the Scripture shows that Paul was already converted at his baptism it would mean that it was an outward act signifying what had already happened within.

In Acts 22:8 Paul called Jesus 'Lord', surely something he would not have done until there had been a change of heart. Second, Ananias called Saul 'brother.' This of course could have been used in the sense of a brother Israelite, although it is very doubtful if Ananias would have called Saul this knowing all that he had done in the past. Added to this evidence, the original account in Acts 9 shows that Paul was healed and filled with the Holy Spirit *before* he was baptised. The latter is a clear sign of God's saving work within Paul and so his baptism would have been an outward testimony to what had happened within.

There are some other scriptures we need to note.

For Christ did not send me to baptize, but to preach the gospel, not in cleverness of speech, that the cross of Christ should not be made void (1 Corinthians 1:17).

Paul explains here that he was sent by the Lord to preach the gospel, to bring the message of true salvation to the Gentiles. However, he also clearly says that he was not sent to baptise! I believe that this verse shows beyond any doubt that baptism is not essential for salvation. The way Paul speaks about the two acts shows that baptism is not included in the good news of the gospel. This as we have already seen fits in with his definition of the main declaration of the gospel in 1 Corinthians 15.

And they said, 'Believe in the Lord Jesus, and you shall be saved, you and your household' (Acts 16:31).

Paul, in response to the jailer's impassioned plea, tells him how he can be saved: 'Believe on the Lord Jesus, and you shall be saved.' After complying with this command, the jailer had an obvious change in his attitude to the prisoners. Those that he should be guarding with his life, he takes and washes and bandages their wounds; only then were he and his family baptised. As we have seen throughout this study the basic presentation of the gospel always includes repentance and believing and baptism is only mentioned sometimes. As such it becomes clear what the Lord is saying is essential for salvation.

Jesus answered 'Truly, truly, I say to you, unless one is born of water and the Spirit, he cannot enter into the Kingdom of God' (John 3:5).

Some groups would seek to use the phrase, 'born of water' to show that to be born again we must be baptised. However, it is important to note that Jesus did not say, 'unless a man is born of baptism'. Jesus often spoke figuratively about water (see John 4:14 and 7:38), and there is no reason to believe that he was talking about baptism in John 3. Titus 3:5 also uses the phrase 'the washing of regeneration', but again there is nothing to link this to a specific act of baptism. The context of the verse would seem to rule out any act that we can do. Salvation is not based on our deeds but on God's mercy.

We can sum this section up with another quotation from Bancroft's book.

The Scriptures represent baptism to be, not the means, but only the sign of regeneration. For this reason only believers – that is, perhaps giving credible evidence of being regenerated – were baptized (Acts 8:12). Not external baptism, but the conscientious turning of the soul to God, which baptism symbolizes, saves us (1 Peter 3:21). Some New Testament verses such as Acts 2:38 and Col 2:12 are to be explained upon the principle that regeneration, the inward change, and baptism, the outward sign of that change, were regarded as only different sides or aspects of the same fact and either side or aspect might, therefore be described in terms derived from the other' (E. H. Bancroft, *Christian Theology*, p. 248).

11

Jehovah's Witnesses

Where did they come from?

The forming of the modern-day Watchtower Bible and Tract
Society of the Jehovah's Witnesses began with Charles Taze
Russell in the 1870s. At this time, after a checkered religious
youth, he began studying the Bible. Under the influence of the
Second Adventists he soon was proclaiming 1874 as the date of
the return of Jesus Christ.

1874 did not see the Lord appearing on earth, but not to be
outdone Russell found a new and interesting teaching. He discovered the Greek word *parousia*, meaning the presence of
Christ, and changed his story to say that Christ did come, but
invisibly. However, there was still not long to wait, because the
kingdom of God would now be set up on earth in 1914.

Six thousands copies of the first edition of *Zion's Watch
Tower*, the forerunner of today's *Watchtower*, were printed in
July 1879. At first it was monthly and sometimes bimonthly but
by the early 1900s it was being printed twice a month as it still
is today. The Watchtower Bible and Tract Society was formed
in 1881 and incorporated in 1884.

Russell died in October 1916 having already changed the
date for the start of the kingdom's earthly reign from 1914 to
1915. This was an action that the second president, Joseph

Franklin Rutherford, was going to follow on several occasions. He also caused quite a stir by changing many doctrines that Russell had held dear, resulting in hundreds or maybe even thousands leaving the Society. It is an interesting fact that many major doctrines of the Watchtower Society today stem from the second president, Rutherford, and not from its founder, Russell.

As a result of certain passages in his book, *The Finished Mystery*, Rutherford served a short sentence for espionage in Atlanta Penitentiary. However, his release from prison only served as an opportunity to give a new impetus to the Society. Today, Jehovah's Witnesses are taught that this release from prison on earth in 1918 heralded the first resurrection of the 144,000 to heaven in the same year.

In 1920 the book *Millions Now Living Will Never Die* was published. This predicted the return to earth of the Old Testament princes, to rule over God's kingdom, in 1925. Men such as Abraham, Isaac and Jacob would return to life and be the leaders of the Great Crowd on earth. So sure were they of their return that by 1930 they even had a house prepared for them in San Diego, California.

1914 saw the release of the book *Children*. At the annual convention that year young people were presented with a copy of the book. In a keynote speech they were then instructed to use it on the door-to-door ministry, in the remaining months before Armageddon. The book counselled that whatever happened they should make sure that they did not get married before that battle started.

Since Rutherford's death in 1942 two further presidents have come and gone. First, Nathan Homer Knorr who was largely responsible for making the 'organisational structure' that the Society has today. He was followed by Frederick W. Franz who died in December 1992.

In Franz's years as president the Society has been through several traumas. First came the expectation built up over 1975 as another date for the kingdom of God to be set up on earth. Approximately a quarter of a million Witnesses left the Society when this date proved another disappointment.

Second, the organisation was rocked in the early 1980's when many from the American headquarters left the Society or were disfellowshipped the term the Society use for expulsion. This group included Ray Franz, the president's nephew and one-time member of the governing body. The trouble started when different groups began reading the Bible without the help of Watchtower publications. They started questioning the authority and the teachings of the Society and many found a true relationship with Jesus Christ.

Continuing traumas are often caused today by a hounding from the media because of the Witnesses' refusal to allow blood transfusions. This has led to the deaths of many innocent people.

All these facts, however, may not cause the average Witness immediately to doubt and leave the Society. First, they will usually not listen readily to anyone outside the organisation, and second, they will believe all the explanations given by the governing body. Yet knowing their history, we can lovingly sow doubts concerning the fact that they believe this has been constituted as 'God's sole visible channel on earth today'.

Who are they?

Jehovah's Witnesses are often viewed with suspicion and mistrust but probably over 90% of those that you meet will be sincere and very zealous. They will believe that unless you become a Witness you will not be in Jehovah's new kingdom.

Most are in the Society for genuine and positive reasons. Often they joined at a time of crisis in their life. Many would have cried out, 'Oh God, help me!' A few days later there would be a knock at the door and two very pleasant Witnesses would begin to bring God's answer. They would have found loving, caring people who would spend many hours explaining the Bible to them.

What they did not realise, though, as they started on their round of five hours of meetings, two to three hours on the doors, and several hours of preparation each week, was that they were losing their own identity. Many did not realise what the subtle process of questions and answers from the Society's own literature was doing to them. Through the teaching that the only people who really hear God are the governing body and that independent thinking is of the devil, individuals stop thinking for themselves and become 'organisational robots'.

Average Witnesses do not think for themselves in any area of life – they simply check what the governing body has written in the latest *Watchtower*, or *Awake!* magazines or in the latest book released. In this way they have no personal relationship with Jesus – only with the 'organisation'. However as they equate serving the 'organisation' with serving Jehovah, this does not present a problem to them.

Their commitment to 'Jehovah's organisation'/Jehovah is total and puts some Christians to shame. They do not see refusing blood transfusions as wasting a life but rather as laying down their life for Jehovah's sake.

What do they believe?

There is only one *God*, the Father and Creator. His name is Jehovah and all true Christians will use this, his personal name. He alone is to be worshipped. In the early church he had one *organisation* with its governing body in Jerusalem. Today he will only have one organisation, the Watchtower Bible & Tract Society with its governing body.

Jesus is unique in that he is the first created being of Jehovah. He is not eternal and as such he cannot be God although he is a lesser god. As their translation of John 1:1 shows, he is 'a god', whereas Jehovah is the God. They also believe that Jesus is only ever called mighty but Jehovah is referred to as almighty. Other verses, especially in the New Testament, eg Revelation 3:14, are mistranslated to show that Jesus is created. Jesus is also the same person as Michael the archangel. Wherever we read in Scripture that Michael did something, it is the same as reading that Jesus did it. After he created Jesus, Jehovah used him to create all other things.

The *Holy Spirit* is a force and extension of the power of Jehovah. He is not a person but an 'it' and is often likened to electricity. The conclusion is therefore that he is not even a person and he certainly cannot be God. Gifts of the Holy Spirit are not for today and anyone manifesting them must have received the enabling from Satan and not God.

The *Trinity*, as can be clearly seen from the above beliefs, must be a pagan doctrine of the 3rd or 4th century. It is not taught in the Bible and none of the early church fathers ever mentioned it. Any Christian who believes in the Trinity is actually part of the 'worldwide empire of Babylon', Satan's kingdom. This is one reason Jehovah's Witnesses believe that everything that goes on inside a church is of the devil.

Jehovah's Witnesses will believe that their doctrine is the true teaching of the *Bible*. However, their translation, the New World Translation, although being 80–90% the word of God, has twisted many key verses. Just about every verse that shows the deity of Christ has been altered and they have regularly translated 'in Christ' as 'in *union with* Christ'. There is no justification for this in the Greek as their own Kingdom Interlinear Translation shows, but it does remove the Witness from the necessity of a personal and intimate relationship with Christ.

Although lip-service will be paid to *salvation* by grace the reality is that the organisation provides the salvation in the end. Only active Jehovah's Witnesses in the organisation will survive the battle of Armageddon, the outpouring of God's wrath on the earth. All the rest of the people, including those with a true relationship with Jesus Christ, will be annihilated. *Hell* does not exist and all who are annihilated obviously have no hope of a resurrection.

Theirs is a two-tier salvation. Only the *144,000* will be with Jesus in heaven and the rest, the *Great Crowd* will have eternal life on a paradise earth.

After Armageddon, all who are counted worthy will be *resurrected* (see next point) and given a second chance of salvation on paradise earth. They must be loyal to the directives of the 144,000 and Jesus ruling in heaven. After being obedient for 1,000 years they must then make sure they are not in the group that the Bible says will follow Satan. Even with a second chance the outcome is hardly certain.

Man does not have an *eternal spirit*; at death he ceases to exist and simply becomes a memory to God. If he is a 'worthy one', God will in time remember and resurrect him to have a second chance in the millennium. This act is more akin to recreating as there is nothing actually left to resurrect.

Dates and *chronology* have always been important to the Watchtower Society. Many dates have been suggested for the setting up of God's kingdom on earth but all have proved false. 1914 has always been one of their key dates but it has had different meanings over the years. Originally it was the setting up of the kingdom of God on earth 40 years after Jesus returned invisibly in 1874. Today it is the actual date for the invisible return of Jesus Christ to take his throne in the heavens. It is also now the end of the Gentile Times and the beginning of the time of the end. As well as this, the generation that saw 1914 will not totally pass away until Armageddon comes.

Other beliefs that should be mentioned include the fact that they do not celebrate Christmas, Easter or birthdays. Jesus did not die on the cross but a stake. God forbids blood transfusions.

Most likely meeting points

The Jehovah's Witnesses aim to call at every door in the country at least once a year. In densely populated areas it may be more frequent. Each Kingdom Hall is equipped with a large map of their area and good organisation to accomplish this task.

The most likely place therefore that you will meet the Witness is on your doorstep. This is good for you because it's 'home territory' and you can be relaxed about witnessing.

Witnesses rarely advertise but they do from time to time come into High Streets and shopping complexes and offer their *Watchtower* and *Awake*! magazines in return for a donation.

Sharing the gospel

I hope by now we have seen that the Witness on our doorstep is a divine appointment rather than a perishing nuisance. The least we can do is bring the conversation around to our testimony of Jesus. However, please do not talk about your salvation so that the Witness can dismiss it as an emotional experience. Wherever possible relate your experience to the commands and promises found in God's word.

We will give just a couple of examples of how conversations could go. The wording may not be exactly what is said but you should get the drift and be ready to come in at the right time.

WITNESS: Are you aware what a terrible state the world is in? It is just as the Lord said in Matthew 24 . . .

CHRISTIAN: Yes, I know Satan is causing many problems for humanity today, but Jesus has told us that we do not need to be over-come by fear. He has said that he gives us peace and victory. Please let me explain what happened in my life . . .

WITNESS: It is interesting that you said you attend the local church. It is good to find those interested in spiritual things today.

However, we do have to be careful that we are receiving the right teaching. For instance so many churches today teach the doctrine of the Trinity but did you know that this booklet clearly shows that it is a pagan doctrine? It is illogical isn't it, how can Jesus be the same as Jehovah?

CHRISTIAN: I do believe the Bible teaches the doctrine of the Trinity, although I do not think that this is the main problem. Did you know that the Bible tells us that God accepts us on what we think of Jesus? Do you agree?

WITNESS: Our view of Jesus is important but not as important as what we think of Jehovah.

CHRISTIAN: Okay. But we show what we think of Jehovah the Father by obeying his instructions. Note what Jehovah says we should think of Jesus (point out relevant scriptures, eg Matt 17:5). I would also like to tell you what happened when I came to know Jesus as Jehovah wants us to . . .

Young Christians may not be able to do anything more at this stage. However, for more mature Christians, to go on to give a simple presentation like the following will be very helpful for the Witness.

Could we look at John 20:28 please? This is the second time that Jesus has appeared to the disciples but the first time that Thomas sees him. In verse 27 Jesus is encouraging him to believe and Thomas' immediate response is to acknowledge Jesus as my Lord and my **God**. (This seems fairly clear until we realise what the Witness had been taught. The Society say that either Thomas got so excited he blasphemed or he said, my Lord looking at Jesus, and my God, looking up to Jehovah in heaven.)

Could we look at the verse carefully please? First, it clearly says Thomas said to him (Jesus) both statements. Second, the Watchtower Greek Interlinear Version (KIT) shows the words

· Thomas used. He said *ho theos* and the literal English rendering underneath is 'the God of me'.

This is the Greek phrase that the Watchtower Society say is used exclusively of Jehovah God. Jesus is called not just 'a god' but 'the God'. If this were not true he would have had to rebuke Thomas in John 20:29. Instead he commends all those who will believe the same as Thomas believed. Notice please that this verse 28 is sandwiched between 27 and 29 both of which encourage belief. What would all the apostles have believed from these words?

First, we have established that the Jesus of the Bible is different from the Jesus of the Watchtower. Now we must also establish that we need a different relationship with Jesus. To do this we turn to John 3:3.

Immediately the Witness will dismiss this verse as just for the 144,000 heavenly ones, but let's look again carefully at the verse.

First get the Witness to read the end of the verses in the Watchtower Bible (NWT) – 'see the kingdom of God'. Most Witnesses will actually translate it in their minds as, 'enter the kingdom of heaven' because it is the 144,000. Make the point though that the verse says 'see the kingdom of God' and ask, 'Don't you expect to see the kingdom of God?'

Every Witness has the hope that they will see the kingdom on earth. This then is for you isn't it? But what has to happen to see the kingdom – we must be born again!

The Witness will not like thinking about being born again because it's only for the 144,000 and if anyone else claims it then it must be some 'voodoo' act. Use illustrations such as the caterpillar and the butterfly and remind them that they do know of people (the remnant of the 144,000 on earth) who are to be born again. Show that to be born again is an act that enables them to live in a new dimension in God's heavenly kingdom. It's no 'voodoo' experience but a work of God in our lives, which is necessary if we are to see God's kingdom.

Finally point out that their Bible says 'unless anyone'. Are you an anyone? If this is only for the 144,000 then God is a liar when He says 'anyone'. What is the only way you will ever see the kingdom of God – earthly or heavenly?

There are many other ways that we can bring Jesus to the Jehovah's Witness and details of other helps will be found in the 'Conclusion' chapter. The important thing is that we spend some time preparing our notes now so that we are ready when the knock, knock arrives.

12

Latter-Day Saints

Where did they come from?

The Church of Jesus Christ of the Latter-day Saints or Mormons as they are more often known had their beginnings in the north of New York State in the early 1800s. A fourteen-year-old boy by the name of Joseph Smith received a vision of Jesus and his Father.

The story goes that there was revival in the churches all around and Joseph wanted to know which church to join. Determined to find the answer, he went into the forest to ask God to tell him which church was right. He received the unexpected response that all churches were apostate and that he was not to join any of them but rather he should start his own. Thus began The Church of Jesus Christ of the *Latter-day* Saints, contrasting with the *former-day* saints that Mormons believe went into complete apostasy. The church that began with the pouring out of the Holy Spirit at Pentecost failed. Joseph Smith became the founding prophet of the only true church on earth today.

The official version of the beginnings of Mormonism is found in *The Pearl of Great Price*. However, problems arise because of several other Mormon-verified versions of the first vision. Discrepancies between these versions include what age was Joseph when he received the vision. Whom did he see? The Lord of glory, two unidentified persons, angels, or the Father and the Son? How many persons were there, one or two? Was there a revival in progress in the area or not? All these problems have led to questioning the very foundations of Mormonism.

All this cannot be dismissed as insignificant because the first vision is very important to Mormons. The following quotations from their own books show this.

The church stands or falls on the reality of this first vision. Joseph Fielding Smith (*Doctrines of Salvation*, Vol. 1, p. 188).

This vision was the most important event that had taken place in all world history since the day of Christ's ministry (Bruce McConkie, *Mormon Doctrine*, p. 284).

The golden plates

This first vision is said to have taken place in 1820 but it was not until 1823 that the next stage took place. In that year Joseph had a further heavenly visitation, telling him about the existence of the golden plates that contained what we know today as the *Book of Mormon*. On the following day he located the plates but was not allowed to take them home until September 1827 when the real work began. Although it took about a year to translate the *Book of Mormon*, most of the work was completed in the last three months when Oliver Cowdrey was helping Joseph. Until then Joseph had two other helpers in the translation work, Emma, his wife, and Martin Harris.

Translating 'God's book' was not without its problems. *Doctrine and Covenants* 3:9,10 tells of God's displeasure with Joseph Smith because he lost 116 pages of the original trans-lated manuscript of the *Book of Mormon*. Martin Harris lost the pages but he thought that Joseph could just retranslate them. The truth was undoubtedly that Joseph could not be sure that it would be the same text if the missing pages were ever found. However, God answered the problem by leading him to another section of the plates that dealt with the same period but in a more spiritual way!

The contents of the Book of Mormon

The *Book of Mormon* is the story of a Hebrew prophet, Lehi, whom the Lord ordered to flee from Jerusalem. He left with his family around 600 BC and they found their way to a new land that is today known as America. Later the descendants of two of Lehi's sons, the Nephites and the Lamanites, fought each other. The Lamanites had departed from the Lord but the Nephites remained faithful and had kept a detailed history of their dealings. Mormon, one of the last remaining Nephites wrote an account of their history on the golden plates and gave them into the hands of his son Moroni. Moroni buried them in the Hill Cumorah, near Palmyra, New York around AD 438, to prevent them from falling into the hands of the Lamanites. He was hiding from the Lamanites at the time and expected to be killed soon after he had buried the plates.

The producing of the Book of Mormon

Mormons will claim that producing the *Book of Mormon* in such a short time itself proves that it is from God and not from man. However there are many other theories that do not include God's help. One suggestion is that the manuscript of a book stolen from the printers became the basis of the story. Another is that, as his mother related, Joseph used to spin great yarns that kept the family enthralled, and so it was a natural talent. Both could be part of the explanation. What is certain is that the *Book of Mormon* contains some 27,000 words from the *King James Version* of the Bible. This shows that using other manuscripts would not be out of the question.

We should probably not rule out some supernatural help

either, but from which source? Smith himself admitted using a peepstone (a type of crystal-ball) to try to find buried treasure. David Whitmer, who was closely involved with the work of producing the *Book of Mormon*, and Joseph's wife Emma both confirmed that Joseph used a peepstone in a hat to accomplish the translation. The supernatural help through the peepstone would not come from God.

The authenticating of the Book of Mormon

As the *Book of Mormon* contains such detailed history it should not be difficult to prove the truth of the book through archaeology, geography, etc. Unfortunately for modern-day Mormons there is little if any evidence in these fields that can be used to support the *Book of Mormon*.

For instance Alma 11:4-19 mentions eight different coins but not one example of even one of them has ever been discovered. Ether 9:18-19 mentions several animals, traces of which have never been found in that place at that time. Indeed two animals mentioned, the cureloms and cumoms have never been discovered, anywhere, or at any time.

From New York to Salt Lake City

While the translating work was continuing the headquarters of the Mormons were first briefly in New York and then in Pennsylvania before they moved to Kirtland, Ohio in 1831. The State of Missouri became known as the land of Zion and the first Mormon temple site was dedicated there in August 1831 and finally opened in 1836.

Continual persecution forced the church to leave Missouri and they settled in Commerce, Illinois in 1839. The town of Commerce was renamed Nauvoo and the Mormons experienced rapid growth but not without problems. In 1844 several discontented members printed charges of polygamy and strange doctrines against Joseph Smith and the Mormon church, in the

Nauvoo Expositor. Enraged, Joseph Smith incited a mob to destroy the printing press and this led to his arrest and imprisonment in the Carthage town jail. Joseph Smith died in a gunfight while trying to break out of jail on 27 June 1844.

Under Brigham Young the Mormons continued west until they reached what today is known as Utah. Here they settled and built Salt Lake City that is still their very impressive headquarters today.

In 1837 the first Mormon converts were recorded in Britain. They were baptised in Liverpool and that town along with Bristol became strong centres in the early days. Many families left through the ports to go to the USA. Today the Mormons claim to be one of the fastest growing cults in Britain, with approximately 120,000 members.

At present there is only one temple in Britain on the borders of Surrey and Sussex but a new one is being built near Chorley. The temple is where their secret ceremonies take place and is different from the regular meeting places you see in many towns.

Who are they?

Mormons will, for the most part, be genuine and believe what they say, but they will be deceived themselves. Many you meet will be Americans, undertaking their two-year missionary service.

At some point they will probably have been given a *Book of Mormon* and asked to read certain verses. They will then have been told to pray and ask God to confirm that this is the word of God. Many at that point will feel the 'burning in the bosom' and receive the testimony that Mormonism is true and Joseph Smith is the prophet. This 'spiritual' experience will often take precedence over any number of facts revealed to them.

Comparatively few Mormons, will have gone through special

temple ceremonies and received 'holy underwear' containing masonic symbols although all the missionaries do so. Maybe they will have been sealed in marriage for eternity or have been baptised for dead relatives. To them Mormonism is the only true religion and the only way to God.

What do they believe?

Before we can look at what they believe we need to understand how they arrive at these beliefs. We will therefore deal with the section on the *Bible* first.

Mormons have three books that they call Scriptures, the *Book of Mormon*, *Doctrine and Covenants* and the *Pearl of Great Price*. They will also quote the Bible and will produce reference editions that are cross linked to the Bible. However, where the Bible and the *Book of Mormon* disagree their eighth Article of Faith makes it clear which they will choose.

> We believe the Bible to be the word of God *as far as it is translated correctly*; we also believe the *Book of Mormon* to be the word of God. (Emphasis added.)

Many Mormons will say that they accept the *King James Version* of the Bible. However, the front cover of the handout edition of the *Book of Mormon* has in big gold letters, 'Another Testament of Jesus Christ'. Why do we need another? What has this Testament added that was not in the original?

Twice in *Doctrine and Covenants* (20:8,9 & 27:5) we read that the fullness of the gospel is found within the *Book of Mormon*. This means that the *Doctrine and Covenants* and the *Pearl of Great Price* can only expand on the *Book of Mormon* but cannot add anything. However, as we will show most of their major doctrines are not found within the *Book of Mormon* and some are even contradicted by it.

Mormons will explain this by progressive revelation through the Living Prophet of the church. The Living Prophet can speak fresh 'scripture', thus adding to or indeed taking away from the revelation up to that point. Many changes have been made to Mormonism since the *Book of Mormon* first appeared. Even the *Book of Mormon* has undergone nearly 4,000 changes since the first 'inspired' edition, approximately 150 years ago.

The Mormon will try to 'prove' that the *Book of Mormon* should be held up alongside the Bible by showing that the Bible foretold the *Book of Mormon*. Ezekiel 37:15-20, they say, shows that the *Book of Mormon* is one of the joined rods, the other rod being the Bible. However, this is an interpretation because the Bible clearly shows that they are rods not books. With such a foundation for their belief in what is scripture it will not be a surprise to find the mixture of their teachings today.

God was once a man. This is one of their teachings not found in the *Book of Mormon* but it is found in Joseph Fielding Smith, *The Teaching of the Prophet Joseph Smith*, pp. 344/5.

This belief alone shows that the Mormon idea of God is unscriptural but because of the Christian words and ideas they use it may at first appear Christian. One God, who was once a man, and not a trinity is not only denied by the Bible but also by the *Book of Mormon*.

For I know that God is not a partial God, neither a changeable being; but he is unchangeable from all eternity to eternity (Moroni 8:18).

. . . And now, behold, this is the doctrine of Christ, and the only and true doctrine of the Father, and of the Son, and of the Holy Ghost, which is one God, without end. Amen (2 Nephi 31:21).

. . . the Father, and the Son, and the Holy Ghost are one; and I am in the Father, and the Father in me, and the Father and I are one.

And thus will the Father bear record of me, and the Holy Ghost will bear record unto him of the Father and me; for the Father, and I, and the Holy Ghost are one (3 Nephi 11:27, 36).

Despite this clear teaching from the *Book of Mormon* they do not just deny the Trinity; they add that all men can become gods. Again this is found in *The Teachings of the Prophet Joseph Smith*, pp. 346/7 but denied by the *Book of Mormon*.

God lives near the planet Kolob according to Bruce McConkie *Mormon Doctrine*, p. 428. In the same way every Mormon man exalted to godhood will receive his own planet to rule over.

Jesus in the spirit realm was the brother of Lucifer. He became an ordinary man was married while he lived on earth and had several children.

Now, remember from this time forth, and for ever, that Jesus Christ was not begotten by the Holy Ghost (Brigham Young, *Journal of Discourses*, Vol. 1, p. 51).

Jesus is talked about especially in Christian countries but the key to Mormonism is not Jesus Christ. The central figure is Joseph Smith as the following quotation from the missionaries' preparation guide to home studies shows.

The main focus of this discussion should be the *Book of Mormon* and the Prophet Joseph Smith . . . After the discussion, the investigators' strongest impression should be of the *Book of Mormon* and the Prophet Joseph Smith.

The Holy Spirit is regarded as a force and not as a person nor as part of the Godhead.

There are writings within Mormonism that show that the death of Jesus Christ is not sufficient for salvation.

It is true that the blood of the Son of God was shed for sins through the fall and those committed by men, yet men can commit sins which it can never remit (Brigham Young, *Journal of Discourses*, Vol. 4, p. 53).

The Mormon scriptures also show very clearly that their salvation is by works and not by faith alone.

. . . it is by grace that we are saved, *after all we can do* (2 Nephi 25:23).
We believe that through the Atonement of Christ, all mankind may be saved, *by obedience to* the laws and ordinances of the Gospel (*Third Article of Faith*).

Not a Mormon alive knows every law and ordinance but some that they will seek to obey are:

The word of wisdom This is found in *Doctrine & Covenants* 89 and it actually forbids strong drinks, hot drinks, and tobacco. In modern-day belief this has been changed to forbidding the drinking of tea, coffee and caffeine drinks. Mormons must abide by the Word of Wisdom to prove themselves worthy of great joy in the next life. (See Study Guide 4 – *Eternal Progression*).

Secret temple ceremonies Not every Mormon is allowed to go to the temple, only those who are found worthy and have received their 'Temple Recommend'. This is a signed pass, valid for one year, which allows the holder into any temple in the world.

Baptism for the dead This instruction is found in *Doctrine & Covenants* 128:17,18. First you must undertake genealogy work to discover the names of your dead relatives. This has led many Mormons into occultic experiences because they are concentrating on the dead. Mormons still claim, especially to Christians, that 1 Corinthians 15:29 is their authority for baptising the dead.

Investigation shows that the *Book of Mormon* disagrees with this belief. Alma 34:34,35 tells us that everything is decided before death and so baptism for the dead is futile. Added to this 2 Nephi 28:22,23 shows that there is no opportunity to be saved after death because then comes the judgement.

Tithing This teaching found in *Doctrine & Covenants* 119:4 is vital if a Mormon wants to go through the temple and receive his exaltation to godhood. Accurate records are kept of every penny given. With special tithing funds etc. Mormons often give up to 30% of their income to the church.

In the Mormon *afterlife* there are three heavens described in *Doctrine & Covenants* 131. The Celestial kingdom is reserved exclusively for those who believe and are obedient to the Mormon gospel. Only those in this kingdom have any hope of becoming gods and ruling over their own planet. Many Mormon men are striving to be in such a position.

The Terrestrial kingdom is the second level and it is reserved for good men and women of all religions, who have not embraced Mormonism. All the wicked and degraded will inhabit the lowest level called the Telestial kingdom. Clearly there are two salvations, a general one for all 'good' people and a specific one for the 'elite' of Mormonism.

Currently *polygamy* is not an official doctrine of the Latter-day Saints, but many believe it will be in the future. Evidently they only gave it up 'officially' because of the law of the land. Their eternal future still involves being a god of a planet with many goddess wives. What needs to be underlined, though, is that according to the *Book of Mormon* polygamy should never have been accepted in the first place.

Behold David and Solomon truly had many wives and concubines, which thing was abominable before me, saith the Lord (Jacob 2:24).

Mormons do not look upon themselves as just another denomination, but uniquely and completely *the Church* of Jesus Christ.

> All other churches are entirely destitute of all authority from God . . . And any person who shall . . . receive a holy ordinance of the gospel from the ministers of any of these apostate churches will be sent down to hell with them (Apostle Orson Pratt, *The Seer*, p. 255).

Non-Mormons will be forever barred from the close presence of God. They lack the required certificate with the authorising signature!

> From the day the Priesthood was taken from the earth to the wind-up scene of all things, every man and woman must have the certificate of Joseph Smith as a passport to their entrance into the mansion where God and Christ are (Brigham Young, *Journal of Discourses*, Vol. 7, p. 289).

Eventually this must result in a direct challenge to Jesus Christ because he is not enough. Without Joseph Smith, the church he founded, the *Book of Mormon*, the temple ritual, the observance of all Mormon church regulations, including the daily wearing of the sacred underwear, the presence of God will be denied us. It is not enough to believe in the Lord Jesus Christ, receive him as personal Saviour, and seek to live according to the teachings of the Bible.

> Full salvation is attained by virtue of knowledge . . . Without continuous revelation . . . there would be no salvation. If it had not been for Joseph Smith and the restoration, there would be no salvation. There is no salvation outside The Church of Jesus Christ of Latter-day Saints (*Doctrines of Salvation*, Vol. 2. quoted by Bruce McConkie, *Mormon Doctrine*, 1988, p. 670).

It is important to know that many of these doctrines will not be revealed when the Mormon first calls at the door but all the above points are clearly documented in Mormon literature.

Most likely meeting points

Some Mormons still call from door-to-door and therefore you may find them on your doorstep, but there will be many parts of the country where this will not happen.

Specific contacts are sought these days and most do not just call 'cold'. Advertising in *Readers' Digest*, TV magazines, etc produces the required names and addresses. The advertisements usually offer the *Book of Mormon* as a companion version to the Bible. Alternatively they offer a message on cassette tape, but both will have an invitation to write for a free copy. Whatever is offered it will not be sent by post but will be delivered personally.

Another place you might meet the Mormons is in your local shopping centre, conducting a questionnaire. The questions asked will vary, depending on the time of year or national events taking place. Finally, you will be asked a question that suggests that if there was something better, surely you would want to hear about it. An appointment would then be made to visit you.

Once in your home the missionaries will want to take you through an introductory course of six lessons. These will reveal what they want you to know, at that point, about Mormonism.

Sharing the gospel

As Mormons are clearly working for their salvation, do find ways of emphasising the grace of God. Remember, though, when talking with them, that they have been taught that Joseph Smith and the *Book of Mormon* are to be the central themes of their discussions. Jesus Christ, however, is still the only way to

God and we need to find ways to talk about him. There are many relevant ways to do this and here is one suggestion using the *Book of Mormon*.

Set the scene by showing that the *Book of Mormon* teaches that the Bible is true and contains the Gospel.

> . . . I beheld other books, which came forth by the power of the Lamb, from the Gentiles unto them, unto the convincing of the Gentiles and the remnant of the seed of my brethren, and also the Jews scattered upon the face of the earth, that the records of the prophets and of the twelve apostles of the Lamb are true. And the angel spake unto me, saying: These last records, which thou hast seen among the Gentiles, shall establish the truth of the first . . . (1 Nephi 13:39-40).

You could also add that it teaches that new birth is essential,

> And now behold, I ask you, my brethren of the church, have ye spiritually been born of God? Have you received his image in your countenances? Have ye experienced this mighty change in your hearts? (Alma 5:14).

> For, said he, I have repented of my sins, and have been redeemed of the Lord; behold I am born of the Spirit . . . I am born of God (Mosiah 27:24, 28).

This surely contradicts their *Third Article of Faith*, which as we have already shown, teaches that the Mormon gospel is one of keeping commandments and ordinances. These words are also contrary to the gospel that Paul preached which is endorsed by the *Book of Mormon*, which is very strange because we read in *Doctrine & Covenants* 18:9 that early Mormons were, 'called even with that same calling with which he (Paul) was called.' Obviously they also must have believed what Paul believed.

Paul tells us that he believes (1 Corinthians 15:1-4) that the gospel is all about Jesus. 1 Corinthians 1:14-17 also shows clearly that baptism was not in the true gospel Paul preached, and Galatians 1:6-10 shows what he said about any other gospel.

Highlight these differences especially in the area of grace and works. Present what you know about the grace of Jesus (2 Corinthians 8:9) and that we cannot do even *one* thing to receive salvation (Ephesians 2:8-9.)

In the light of these differences and because only one can be preaching the truth, ask if together you could answer the following questions from the *Book of Mormon* and the Bible.

Are we justified by the law?

2 Nephi 2:5, '. . . and by the law no flesh is justified', agrees with Romans 3:20, 'because by the works of the Law no flesh will be justified . . .' The answer is an emphatic no, we are not. Be ready to show (Galatians 3:24) that the purpose of the law is to act as our schoolteacher to lead us to Christ. Ask the Mormon, have the commandments you have been taught led you to Christ?

Do we work for salvation or is it a free gift?

2 Nephi 2:4, '. . . and salvation is free', agrees with Ephesians 2:8-9, 'For by grace you have been saved through faith; and that not of yourselves, it is the gift of God; not as a result of works, that no one should boast.' Salvation is a free gift.

In whom alone do we have salvation?

2 Nephi 31:21, '. . . and there is none other way not name given under heaven whereby man can be saved . . .' agrees with Acts 4:12, '. . . there is no other name under heaven that has been given among men, by which we must be saved'. There is agreement; the only name is Jesus.

Make each point slowly and carefully and ask whether the Bible and the *Book of Mormon* agree. Finally offer a loving challenge to follow this clear testimony of the saving work of Christ alone. Bring this home further by sharing your testimony of new life in Christ.

There must be no adding to the simple and completed gospel of Jesus Christ. This is the solid ground we are encouraged to build on both in the Bible and the *Book of Mormon*.

Short presentation

Time is precious and if you do not have much of it on the next occasion you meet a Mormon, here is a short presentation that is often effective.

Turn to 1 Corinthians 15:29 and ask them if they believe that the true church of Christ today should be baptising for the dead. Let them explain their position and then tell them that you have a few problems over this and could they help you sort them out. Agree with them that the context of 1 Corinthians 15 is resurrection. Just as Paul has had to correct other problems in the Corinthian church he now deals with the fact that some do not believe in the resurrection (15.12). In the correcting of this he mentions those who are baptised for the dead (15.29). However, in the next verse he talks about we, showing that Paul is not saying that the Christian church is baptising for the dead. Paul is emphasising that those, the pagans in Corinth, are doing it. His argument is that even the pagans believe there is a resurrection of the dead, so how much more should the Christians.

Having explained this, ask the Mormon, 'Why does the Mormon church today, a group that claims to be the only true church, do what the pagans did in Corinth?'

By practising baptism for the dead they have ignored both the teaching of the Bible and the *Book of Mormon* (see earlier,

'What they believe' section). Ask, 'What is your authority for baptising dead people into the Mormon church?' The Bible clearly teaches that there is one life, one death and one judgement. After death it is too late to change one's mind.

13

Worldwide Church of God

Where did they come from?

The Worldwide Church of God is still known by some as *Armstrongism*, after its founder Herbert W. Armstrong. However, with recent developments this title is no longer applicable. Many changes have taken place since Armstrong's death in January 1986.

People will also know this group by the magazine it publishes, *Plain Truth*. Many Christians have read this magazine unaware whom it was produced by. Do not be full of guilt if you are one because lately it is very difficult to find the errors within its pages, but more of that later.

A few years ago you would see racks of the *Plain Truth* magazine outside railway stations etc for free distribution. Today these have largely disappeared and the magazine is sent through the post. This is partly due to financial restraints but it may be also a response to over-zealous Christians who used to take too many, but not to read. At one point this caused the following notices to appear on the racks,

Warning: The magazines on this stand are provided free of charge to all having a genuine wish to read them. Any persons removing the same for other than genuine reasons may commit an *offence* rendering themselves *liable to prosecution*.

Beginnings

The church founded in 1934 was a splinter group from the Church of God (Seventh-day), for whom Herbert Armstrong was a minister. Original roots of the Worldwide Church of God were therefore in the Adventist Movement, similar to the Jehovah's Witnesses.

As the church itself started life as a breakaway group it is hardly surprising that there have been many splinter groups formed by ex Worldwide Church of God members. Most of these still hold the original false teachings of Armstrong and some that you might come across are listed here with the year they were formed and their leader.

The Association of Christian Development, 1974, Kenneth Westby
The Foundation for Biblical Research, 1974, Ernest Martin
Giving and Sharing, 1975, Richard Nickels
Triumph Prophetic Ministries, 1988, William Dankenburg
The Philadelphia Church of God, 1990, Gerald Flurry
The Global Church of God, 1993, Roderick Meredith

The most notable defection, though, must be that of Herbert Armstrong's fourth child, Garner Ted. He was eventually expelled from the Worldwide Church of God in 1978 for alleged immoral conduct. Garner Ted set up his own group, the 'Church of God International', which has a fairly large following in Britain. Although separated from the founding group they still hold to most of the teachings.

There have also been two main breakaways from the Church of God International. The Church of God, Denton Congregation, founded in 1985 by Austin Newell and the

Congregation of God, Seventh day, founded in 1992 by John Pinkston.

Early days

Herbert W. Armstrong was born on 31 July 1892 and died in 1986 at the age of 93. He founded the Worldwide Church of God in January 1934, believing that the 'Sardis' era (Revelation 2&3) of the church had ended and that the 'Philadelphia' era had begun. His belief was that the door that Jesus was opening (Revelation 3:8) was a door to the mass media of radio and the printing press. Through these means the original gospel of Christ would be preached. He fully believed that no church had preached the gospel of Christ since Jesus did it himself on earth. Many groups had preached about the gospel but the Worldwide Church of God would be the first to truly preach it.

As an advertising salesman Armstrong knew the potential of media exposure and today despite many changes the organisation keeps to this policy. However, this is not without problems in the current financial climate and the seeming lack of growth in the membership of the church. January 1991 saw the demise of their theological magazine *Good News*. *Plain Truth* has also dropped from its largest distribution of over 7,000,000 copies per issue to just over 3,000,000. TV stations in America taking their programme *The World Tomorrow* have also halved since 1988, but it is still broadcast to Britain and Europe via satellite.

Early influence on the Worldwide Church of God was via Armstrong's contact with the Adventist group. As such they were convinced that salvation came only by keeping the commandments. Their message was a mixture of Old Testament law and British Israelism with an added sprinkling of errors such as denial of both the Trinity and the existence of hell. Armstrong's authoritarian leadership helped develop the church along these lines. It is reported that he lived in luxury while many of his followers lived on or below the poverty level trying to pay all the tithes that the church demanded.

False prophecies were another controversial area for Armstrong. The two books, *1975 In Prophecy* and *The United States and British Commonwealth in Prophecy* are full of clearly documented false predictions given in the name of the Lord. This is one of the tests that prove that the Worldwide Church of God is not God's true and only church.

The current leadership is seeking to 'clean up' the act of the church as far as these prophecies are concerned. We should remember however that they were given in God's name by the founder of the church. If he is now being branded as a false prophet, the Worldwide Church of God has no true foundation. What is happening reminds me of second president Rutherford's about-turns after taking over from Russell the founder of the Watchtower Bible and Tract Society. Armstrong has been openly criticised in the *Worldwide News*, 21 May 1990, p. 6, for many things he did wrong but especially for false prophecy.

Modern developments

As indicated already there have been many changes to the church since Armstrong's death in 1986. Herbert Armstrong is still accredited as the founder of the Worldwide Church of God but the publisher is now Joseph W. Tkach. He is the new chief man watching over the editing of *Plain Truth* and taking all leadership decisions of the organisation. Changes he has made to *Plain Truth*, and to the beliefs of the group, are a 'Christianising' process. Current issues of *Plain Truth* contain very little controversial material and indeed it is not always possible to discover any erroneous teaching. Last year a member of my fellowship gave me a copy. She said she knew the group was wrong but please could I show her where these errors were in that issue. It took much careful searching and a knowledge of the 'cultese' language to find the errors.

With all the changes there are some things that never alter. The life of founder Herbert Armstrong was investigated thoroughly and many discrepancies were found between what he claimed and what actually happened. Tkach has been subjected to the same scrutiny and again his life does not live up to his claims. Investigations were carried out by an ex-member group in Pasadena, California who produce a news-sheet entitled *Ambassador Report* and several areas of his life raised serious questions.

Despite this Tkach remains in charge and what became clear very quickly was that the Worldwide Church of God under his leadership was destined to go through radical changes. As early as December 1990 it was reported that Tkach had changed 26 of Armstrong's doctrines and policies. This 1991 quotation gives clear evidence that it was continuing.

. . . those now requesting the WCG [Worldwide Church of God] booklet *The United States and Britain in Prophecy* are being informed that the booklet is no longer in print. And WCG public relations man Michael Snyder has predicted that within a year the doctrine found in that booklet will probably no longer be taught by the WCG . . . Official church spokesman Michael Snyder, interviewed on the religious radio program *Talk From the Heart* (broadcast Dec. 13 on WMUZ, Detroit), stated that **all** WCG doctrines are under review . . . With Tkach Sr., Michael Feazell, and Tkach Jr. making the WCG's public image their top priority, and with WCG public relations man Michael Snyder busily cooperating with mainstream Christian media around the world, it's no wonder so many think the WCG has become a nice organization (*Ambassador Report*, May 1991, p. 1).

Through the 1990s the Worldwide Church of God has continued to undergo drastic changes and they are probably not finished yet.

Some changes have brought confusion; for instance it was widely reported in America from sources within and outside the church that the doctrine of the Trinity was officially accepted at a conference in June 1993. Yet some parts of the church appear to be denying this.

Some observers feel that these changes move the Worldwide Church of God towards mainstream Christianity and they should be removed from the cult list. I for one feel it is far too early to do this. *Ambassador Report* clearly shows that there is still a need to look beyond some apparent cosmetic changes.

Today if one reads only the WCG (Worldwide Church of God) publications intended for the general public, one can easily be led to believe that the WCG is just one more Protestant denomination . . . But carefully read these WCG writings aimed at only the baptised members of the WCG and one can clearly see that the WCG still retains all the key traits of a 'destructive cult'. For example, the February 25, 1992 Tkach letter to his members and co-workers . . . was very plain: As I write this month, I pray that God's people truly understand what it means to be a member of the body of Christ, and why it is that the Worldwide Church of God holds certain distinctive teachings and practices not followed by most other churches . . . That is why this Church stresses obedience to God as necessary to Christianity . . . What makes us the true Church of God? We are God's Church because God works in us by his Spirit to worship him and serve him. It is what God does that makes us his Church . . . Does this mean it makes no difference what Church you belong to? Far from it! It makes every difference, for you need to be part of Christ's body (*Ambassador Report*, June 1993, p. 8).

Other apparent changes will be listed in the relevant sections of 'What they believe', but as with most groups that go through such radical changes there are many people who became dissatisfied along the way. One of the most interesting of these has been Michael Snyder, the Public Relations man for the Worldwide Church of God for many years. Often he defended the policy of the church to the media, as we have already seen. Since then he has left and initially went into hiding but it is reported from 'reliable sources' that he now believes this group to be a cult.

Who are they?

Until any changes really take affect within the church they are a very secretive people. With their belief in the Old Testament Law they would meet on Saturdays in rented buildings. These meetings would not be advertised and unless you lived near one of their halls you would probably not know there was a spiritual gathering. Outsiders walking in would not be welcome as you would need to be vetted before you could attend.

Active members would have started with the *Plain Truth* magazine and then probably moved on to the Bible Study Course and other publications. Next they would write and enquire about groups or individuals near them and that is when they would receive a visit from the local leader.

There is some indication that this is changing and I have received invitations to a couple of open meetings near me. However, old habits appear hard to change and we are still receiving reports of exclusiveness and secrecy in other parts of the country.

What do they believe?

As the belief of this group is changing rapidly, we will try to show both the historical belief and what some of the new changes mean. An American, Dave Pack, has compiled a list of 154 doctrinal changes and 28 policy changes, published in the *Ambassador Report*, September 1993.

To Armstrong **God** was the creator and the one whom we should serve even if in Old Testament style. However, he obviously was not all-supreme because we could all become gods and join the family. In the church's publication we read, 'You are setting out on a training to become creator – to become God!' *Why Were You Born?*, p. 225.

Under the section on the Trinity we will show that this does not appear now to be possible because one doctrinal change listed is that God is only adopting us and we will never become gods. Their *Statement of Beliefs* says about God,

God, by the testimony of Scripture, is one divine Being in three eternal, co-essential, yet distinct hypostases (see definition under Trinity), Father, Son and Holy Spirit. He is the only true God, eternal, immutable, omnipotent, omniscient. He is the Creator of heaven and earth, Sustainer of the universes, and Source of human salvation. Though transcendent, God has a direct and personal relationship with human beings. God is love and infinite goodness.

In the past Jesus was a secondary figure but their 1988 book *Who Was Jesus?*, changed all of that. Tkach wrote that he was thrilled at the release of this book, dedicated to teaching people about Jesus. This emphasis is another major change.

The new emphasis on the person of Jesus alters what HWA (Herbert W. Armstrong) taught concerning the church's purpose for existence. For HWA, the primary purpose of the church was not preaching Jesus. HWA taught that the church's primary function was to publish and broadcast the gospel of the coming Kingdom . . .' *Ambassador Report*, September 1989, p. 5. Now the gospel of the kingdom is almost entirely about Jesus.

The first chapter of their 'Jesus' book entitled *Jesus as Man and God* appears to show that they already believed that Jesus was God and part of the Trinity. However, a closer reading of the book shows that first impressions can be misleading. Quoting John 10:30 they state,

> He obviously didn't mean they were one being. They were two separate personalities who thought as one. The word (Jesus) and God were one in co-operation, in thought, in deed, in philosophy. Though they were two distinct individuals they acted in such concert that it was proper to say they were one – a singularity (*Who Was Jesus?*, pp. 17/18).

Jesus was God, the YHWH of Old Testament, who was under God the Father's authority. Together these two members of God's family were discussing.

> the most awesome concept that could ever be conceived. God and the Word are saying, 'Let us re-create ourselves.' To repeat: the plan was to make new members of the God family . . . Finally, obedient and trusting humans would be transformed into very God by a resurrection (*Ibid*., pp. 22, 26).

When this version of the book was released in 1988 we could still become gods and join the God family that presently only has two members. Jesus, although part of this family, does not appear to have always been God.

> The Word literally emptied himself of divine God nature and became the man, Jesus Christ (*Ibid*., p. 35).

The Holy Spirit also appears to be undergoing some changes but exactly where the doctrine will end is not clear.

The Holy Spirit, here, is the essence or power of God. If the Holy Spirit were a person, it would be Christ's father. Here we clearly see that the Holy Spirit is the power of God, much as electricity is a power in the physical realm (*Ibid*., p. 44).

To put the teaching of the *Trinity* in the most up to date context I will quote from a letter received by a member of Reachout from the group's British headquarters in Borehamwood, Herts. If it appears to contradict anything else we have quoted from official church sources, it probably does! The doctrine is still in a state of flux but this seems to be the latest (April 1994) official position at the time of writing.

> The word 'trinity' is not found in the Bible and we will refrain from using it for that reason. It merely means 'threefoldness'. In that sense, we do believe in the 'threefoldness' of God – being the Father, Son and Holy Spirit – and always have. But we do not accept the traditional teaching about the 'Holy Trinity' and never have. We still do not believe that the Holy Spirit is a person and will refrain from using the word 'persons' in reference to the Godhead . . . The Bible does not allow for two, three or four God beings . . . Our teaching is that God is one Being, existing eternally in three hypostases (that without which something cannot be): Father, Son and Holy Spirit . . . To put it briefly, God is one being in three *hypostases* or *permanent* modes of being. In other words, God has revealed himself in three ways of *being* (not in three beings).

The *Bible* is used extensively in the church's literature but it is doubtful if it is their final authority. If it has always been then it means the Bible has changed because their beliefs have changed. They either had to be wrong initially or wrong now or, of course, both. With all the changes it appears it is not Scripture that motivates the church but what the current leadership feels it is expedient to believe.

This is shown by several beliefs that are not biblical. For example, Christ does not have a body; man is not made in the literal image of God; and prehistoric people may have been created by Satan.

The last book that Herbert Armstrong wrote before his death was entitled *The Mystery of The Ages*. In it he claimed that the gospel of Christ was proclaimed in 1953 for the first time in 1900 years.

> Christ's message was Christ's gospel – the gospel of Christ. It had not been proclaimed to the world until the first week in 1953, when for the first time in about 1,900 years – a century of time cycles – it went out on the world's most powerful radio station, Radio Luxembourg in Europe (*Mystery of the Ages*, pp. 241/242).

Interestingly this book was serialised in *Plain Truth* after Tkach took over as editor. This is one claim that has yet to be modified, although he has ordered that the book should not be distributed.

The book goes on to claim that for 1,800 years the world did not know the gospel. Everybody else preached *about* the gospel of Christ but the Worldwide Church of God alone preached the gospel of Christ. This is the gospel that you must believe to be saved.

The emphasis under Tkach has changed. Armstrong saw the importance of being watchmen and warning about the coming power of the Beast. Tkach, however sees the church's commission is now to preach Jesus, which leads us on to the matter of *salvation*. Under Armstrong salvation was a process,

> Salvation, then is a process! But how the God of this world would blind your eyes to that. He tries to deceive you into thinking all there is to it is just 'accepting Christ' with 'no works' – and presto – change, you are pronounced 'saved'. But the Bible reveals that none is yet 'saved' (*Why Were You Born?*, p. 11).

In those days being born again could only happen at the resurrection; now you can be born again at conversion, not wait for the resurrection. Tkach has changed the terminology because you are saved now and do not have to endure to the end.

In the January 28, 1991 issue of the church's newspaper *The Worldwide News* (WN), one of Tkach's ghostwriters, under Tkach's by-line, wrote how WCG (Worldwide Church of God) members are already 'born again'. Summarising the new doctrine, the WN article stated: '. . . when the Bible speaks of a person as being "born again" it is speaking of Christian conversion, not of the ultimate Christian inheritance' (p. 6). While the new WCG position completely contradicts a major HWA (Herbert W. Armstrong) teaching, Tkach's ghostwriter explained that HWA simply didn't understand the subtle difference between the Greek words *gennao* and *sullambano*. But Tkach does, supposedly (*Ambassador Report*, May 1991, p. 1).

Whatever the wording, the fact remains that according to the first edition of *Who Was Jesus?* salvation is still a process that requires 'work' and 'striving' on our behalf.

After living a perfect life in the flesh, he (Jesus) could pay the penalty for all sins, thus erasing *past* human defects (sins) . . . One problem still remained. The human pots could acquire new spiritual defects because of future sin. Jesus as the master spiritual potter had to create minds that strove to keep themselves free from future sin. That's exactly what he does today . . . God could begin calling individuals out of sin. As they strove to submit to him in everything, God would apply Jesus' sacrifice to their lives . . . Salvation is really a four-part plan. First, God must choose a person to become a member of the 'elect' . . . Second, God must apply Jesus' sacrifice to forgive . . . Third . . . That person then strives to overcome his or her human nature in obedience to God . . . Fourth, the 'new person' . . . is, at Jesus' Second Coming, to be changed in composition to immortal spirit as a member of God's family (*Who Was Jesus?*, pp. 24, 25, 39, 42).

Here only the terminology appears to have changed; we still are not sure of our salvation now. Still needing to strive to get rid of what we can never overcome, without knowing Christ's victory on Calvary in our lives now! There is a claim that they now believe that salvation is a free gift and baptism is not required to be saved, but as yet nothing appears to have been officially written down.

Another aspect of salvation that has not changed is that in this age relatively few will be saved. The majority will get a second chance in the new kingdom on earth.

> This can be called the 'Church Age' . . . God has purposed that at this time, only comparatively few individuals should be made part of his Church . . . What is to happen to all those who lived and died throughout the centuries until the Messiah's return – those who weren't yet called? These individuals will be resurrected to physical life after God's kingdom has been on this earth for a thousand years. They will also be given God's Spirit and have an opportunity to receive eternal life (see Rev. 20:4, 11-12). (*Who Was Jesus?*, pp. 40/41).

Other changes in belief worth mentioning include the *cross* that to Armstrong was a phallic symbol of pagan religions is now accepted as a symbol of service and sacrifice. *Plain Truth*, May/June 1993, even contained an article that said that Jesus died on the cross not a stake.

Celebrating certain days appears to be under scrutiny. Now there is nothing wrong with appropriate festive decorations and treats for the kids at Christmas. Easter is recognised as a religious day that is important to Christianity. Birthday parties and celebrations are now acceptable too.

Finally, we should mention that it appears that their belief in British Israelism, so long a pillar of belief in the church, appears to have been abandoned.

Most likely meeting point

As we have already suggested, members of this group have been quite secretive in the past. The main way you would meet them is through correspondence via *Plain Truth* magazine. This is probably still true although they appear to be holding public meetings from time to time and you could be invited to such a gathering.

Sharing the gospel

With all the changes that are going on it is probably unwise to make bold statements of exactly what a member believes. More to the point would be to ask them questions and let them tell you what their current position is.

Asking questions that will begin to sow doubt in their mind as to the validity of the Worldwide Church of God is a great way to start. We have listed some sample questions below and there should be one or two applicable, whatever the current belief of the person you are talking to.

How could Armstrong be God's man to bring in the true gospel when he was a false prophet?

When the doctrines of the WCG are shown false by Scripture who will you believe the WCG or the Bible?

What happens to all those who lived before 1953, when the Bible shows there is no second chance?

With all the changes that have taken place in the gospel of the Worldwide Church of God how could it have been the true gospel in 1953?

Sowing doubt is only half the job and so go on to make some

clear scriptural presentations. Some suggestions for topics and scriptures that show the truth of the statements are found below.

The Scripture shows that no man can become a God – Romans 3:10, 22-23.

Salvation cannot come via adherence to any law – Romans 3:19-24; Galatians 3:10-14; Titus 3:5.

There is only one salvation and it is now available to all people – 2 Corinthians 6:1-2.

Being born again is available for all now. It is not just a few chosen ones – John 3:3.

Days are not important to God – Colossians 2:16.

14

The Unification Church

Where did they come from?

Members of the Unification Church are better known as 'moonies', a nickname derived from the name of their founder, Reverent Sung Myung Moon. Born on 6 January 1920 Moon was raised in a Presbyterian family. Here, as happens with so many cults, the official history of their leader differs from the facts discovered. Officially Moon's family converted to Christianity in 1931 when he would have been eleven years old. Early on Easter Sunday morning 1935, when he would have been just fifteen, it is recorded that Moon received a vision of Jesus Christ. In the vision he was commissioned to further the building of God's kingdom on earth. There followed a period of intense prayer and Bible study through which God is supposed to have shown him important insights and guided him to reinterpret the Scriptures. It is also taught that during this time he discovered until then unknown principles that were the basis for God's work to save humankind.

According also to the official sources of the church, Moon began his ministry to teach these new revelations, in southern Korea in 1945. Feeling he was rejected by those he preached to he left the South and went to Communist-held northern Korea.

Eventually, because of his faith, he was arrested, severely tortured and sent to a concentration camp. Surviving in the appalling conditions, he was eventually liberated in October 1950. Moving to Seoul, it was there he founded the *Holy Spirit Association for the Unification of World Christianity*, in 1954.

Other sources do not necessarily bear out these claims. They show that before Moon's claimed vision of Jesus he had already dabbled in the occult. No mention is made either, in the official version, of his search for the perfect wife that led him through four marriages. Some even claim that the second marriage was never ended legally. Further, no mention is made either of Moon's business empire, as diverse as M-16 rifles and ginseng, reported to be worth millions of pounds. The official record does mention some areas that have brought him respectability. These include ownership of *The Washington Times* and several helpful scientific and cultural exchange forums that he has helped to set up.

No mention is made though of his checkered history between the age of sixteen and the early seventies when he was launched on to the western scene in the USA. Apart from his marriages and a spell in prison for sex offences, it is also reported that Moon has had links with the Korean Central Intelligence Agency and a Japanese organised crime syndicate.

In 1982 Moon was convicted of tax fraud and served a thirteen-month sentence in Danbury's federal penitentiary. During this period 'moonies' were not quite so visible on the street corners in American cities. Their precarious situation had not been helped in Britain either by their losing the *Daily Mail* libel case. This caused them to pull back and even at one point to state publicly they were going to leave Britain. However, this never took place, and they probably never intended to do so. Whether as visible or not they are still at work and many young people are still at risk.

Despite all of the bad publicity and very questionable history, to date over two million people have accepted the invitation and been 'brainwashed' to join the church. Moon has a message that many sceptics like to hear, 'The Cross is the symbol of defeat of Christianity'.

The work today in Britain often revolves around a Unification Study Centre. Young people, especially foreign students, are invited in for a coffee, discussion and to watch videos of Moon's teachings.

Who are they?

It will be helpful if you can understand what the person you meet has been through. As a new recruit they would have attended a series of events to bring their mind under the control of the group. Initially they would have been encouraged to isolate themselves from their family so that all contact from the past is cut off. They would have been 'love-bombed', giving them the feeling of a new home and a new family. Many of them would have been lonely students or travellers away from home for the first time so this would have been very acceptable.

As time went on they may have experienced physical deprivation, exhaustion and intense indoctrination. This indoctrination would be vital to win their complete loyalty. Often they would have been persuaded to hand over all their possessions to the Unification Church.

Probably by the time you meet the 'moonie' they will be totally dependent on Moon and literally worship him. Ex-moonie Steve Hassan reports that,

> Members bow three times with their face touching the floor before an altar with Sun Myung Moon's picture on it and recite a six-point pledge to be faithful to God, to Moon, and to the fatherland – Korea (*Combatting Cult Mind Control*, p. 3).

It is admitted that Moon experimented with occult powers. He had contact with familiar spirits through seances, and condoned mediumistic trances, clairvoyance etc. We should be aware that his followers may also be connected with occultism today.

Members of this group will not just go under the banner of the Unification Church. There is evidence that the following organisations are either owned or set up by them.

International Relief Friendship Foundation (IRFF) – works to relieve suffering and poverty.

International Cultural Foundation (ICF) – promoting academic and scientific exchange.

International Conference on the Unity of the Sciences (ICUS) – annual convention.

Professors World Peace Academy (PWPA) – international body composed of scholars, scientists etc.

Summit Council for World Peace – described as a goodwill organisation promoting friendly relations.

International Religious Foundation (IRF) – dedicated to fostering world peace through religious dialogue.

New Ecumenical Research Association (New ERA) – sponsors conferences on special themes.

Interdenominational Conferences for Clergy (ICC) – seminars bringing together clergy from all denominations.

Assembly of the World's Religions – promoting interreligious understanding.

Religious Youth Service – bringing young people together in practical humanitarian work.

The Collegiate Association for the Research of Principles (CARP) – international student movement.

Sun Hwa Art School – provides general education for 3,600 in Seoul.

The Little Angels – children's entertainment troupe.

Universal Ballet Company.

New York City Symphony Orchestra.

Artists Association International – encourages artists to use their talents for the benefit of humanity.

World Media Association – annual conferences for idea exchanges.

Paragon House – publishing house.

Washington Times – newspaper.

New York City Tribune – newspaper.

Middle East Times – newspaper.

Global Intelligence Digest – magazine.

Insight – magazine.

World & I – magazine.

International Highway Project – international highway literally spanning the world.

What do they believe?

A summary of what Moon teaches will probably be of help before we look at one or two areas in more detail. The heart of this new revelation that Moon had was that Jesus, the second Adam, failed. There was therefore a need for a third Adam, the Messiah, the Lord of the Second Advent. For many years Moon did not publicly declare that he was 'The Messiah', although it was always clear from his writings that he believed it.

> With the fullness of time, God has sent his messenger to resolve the fundamental questions of life and the universe. His name is Sun Myung Moon . . . He fought alone against myriads of satanic forces in both the spiritual and physical worlds, and finally triumphed over them all. In this way, he came in contact with many saints in paradise and with Jesus, and thus brought into Light all the heavenly secrets through his communion with God (*Divine Principle*, p. 16).

Moon further claimed that the Messiah would appear in a physical body, born in the East in an oriental land populated by

Christians. He would also unify all religions – the full name of the movement is *The Holy Spirit Association for the Unification of World Christianity*. His birth would be around 1920 and consequently these clues could only lead you to one man.

In 1992 Moon finally declared publicly that he was the Messiah. However, it went a little beyond that as the report by the Unification Church's own publication shows.

Amidst the splendour of the magnificent Little Angels Performing Arts Centre in Seoul, Rev Sun Myung Moon announced in this speech on August 24, 1992, to a distinguished audience of current and former heads of state, scholars, professors and religious leaders, that he *and Mrs Moon* were the Lord of the Second Coming – the True Parents – the Messiah (*Unification Newsletter*, Vol. 8, No. 1, (Jan 1993), p. 2). (Emphasis added.)

This declaration that both he and his wife were the Messiah underlines the basis of all their teaching, dualism. They look into the world and see male and female, positive and negative, protons and electrons etc. From here they work back and say that the Creator of all this must also contain the + and –, an idea similar to the ancient Chinese yin and yang belief of Taoism. God, to Moon, is therefore both Mother and Father.

As may be expected, 'moonies' do not use the *Bible*, but rather the 536-paged *Divine Principle*. This contains the new revelation received by Moon from Jesus Christ and was first published in 1957. The claim of Moon is that the 'what is to come' mentioned in John 16:13 is the *Divine Principle*. He explains that there are three ages, the Old Testament Age, which used the Old Testament; the New Testament Age, which used the New Testament; and the Completed Testament Age, which uses the *Divine Principle*. The Bible is incomplete, not for this age, therefore the *Divine Principle* is the sole authority of the Unification Church.

It may be displeasing to religious believers, especially to Christians, to learn that a new expression of truth must appear. They believe that the Bible . . . is perfect and absolute in itself. Truth, of course, is unique, eternal, unchangeable, and absolute. The Bible, however, is not the truth itself, but a textbook teaching the truth . . . we must not regard the textbook as absolute in every detail (*Divine Principle*, p. 9).

Just as the Old Testament words lost their light when Jesus and the Holy Spirit came with new Words in order to fulfil the Old Testament Words, so the New Testament Words . . . will lose their light when Christ comes with the new Word, in order to fulfil the New Testament Words (*Divine Principle*, p. 118).

Jesus Christ is definitely not God.

Jesus, being one body with God, may be called a second God (image of God), but he can by no means be God Himself (*Divine Principle*, p. 211).

According to Moon, Christ failed by being killed on the cross before accomplishing his mission. Jesus should have married someone with a perfect relationship with God, had children and thus produced a building block for the perfect society. The cross was not God's original plan, it was actually *'a grievous mistake'*. Moon has come to finish the task that Christ began.

God's intention from the beginning was for man and woman to achieve a perfect and mature relationship with God before having children. If this had happened the mature couple would have had perfect children. Adam and Eve fell before perfection and this resulted in there needing to be a physical salvation as well as a spiritual salvation.

Two salvations were needed because there were two falls. Eve first had sexual relationships with Lucifer, which caused the spiritual fall and then with spiritually immature Adam, which caused the physical fall.

Christ on the cross accomplished the spiritual salvation but not the physical one. Moon the 'third Adam' is going to accomplish the physical redemption by setting up the Perfect Family. It is this belief that leads to the hundreds of arranged marriages we read of in our newspapers.

> The cross cannot completely liquidate our original sin . . . If Jesus had not been crucified . . . He would have accomplished the providence of salvation both spiritually and physically . . . Thus, Christ must come again on the earth to accomplish the purpose of the providence of the physical . . . (*Divine Principle*, pp. 142, 147, 148).

The teaching of Moon that Christ failed would appear to contradict the Old Testament prophecies of Psalm 22 and Isaiah 53 among others. However the way the 'moonies' look at this is very different. They believe that Jesus' life could have had two outcomes, either he could have become the Lord of glory **or** the Lord of suffering. The outcome would depend on humanity's response because God's foreknowledge is limited by man's response. Their belief is that Jesus should have become the Lord of glory not the suffering servant.

Most likely meeting points

Usually you will meet the 'moonie' in the High Street when they move out in teams to sell magazines, flowers etc, although in some areas, they will also come door-to-door.

They will have no problem in lying, claiming they are collecting for whatever charity is in the news, children, drug rehabilitation, the homeless, etc. In their warped thinking they do not look on this lying as wrong because they are claiming money back from someone under Satan's control to be used for

God. They will often have a daily quota of sales that must be achieved before they finish for the day.

There are two other possible areas where you might meet 'moonies'. First, students may be invited to attend debates on relevant subjects at local colleges, organized by CARP. Second, Christians may meet them as they will often attend churches or Christian Unions looking for those who are dissatisfied or have problems.

People who get involved with these groups, whether they are fringe ones or not, stand the risk of being indoctrinated with Unification Church principles.

Sharing the Gospel

Patience and spiritual warfare is needed. We need to remember, however, that our fight is not against the 'moonie' but against the god of this world who has blinded their eyes. The 'moonie' believes that Moon is the Messiah. If we just seek to slander Moon, we will not be helping to draw them out but instead push them further in to the organisation. They are warned, 'Christians of today will be the first to persecute the Messiah at the time of the Second Advent'. *Divine Principle*, p. 533.

We need to ask questions that will begin to sow doubt in their hearts and minds. They are so pressurised and brainwashed that they normally do not have time to think for themselves, but while they are with us, we can give them that time.

Some questions we can ask to help break down their resistance and see things as they are really include,

Why was Moon in jail for sexual perversion?

Why did the perfect marriage take four attempts?

Why does the group that wants to 'unify' hate all Christian churches?

What do you think about Moon being put in jail for tax fraud?

If the *Divine Principle* is the completed Testament, I can

understand it fulfilling the revelation of the Bible but why does it contradict so much?

Ask these questions genuinely and then use the answers to move on to make a positive Biblical presentation related to something already said, wherever possible. Here are a few suggestions and although as we have seen they do not accept the Bible as God's word, they do use facts from it in their theology. The areas raised can be looked at in the context of Moon's teaching.

As God's word will never pass away (Isaiah 40:8 and Matthew 24:35), surely the 'what is to come' of John 16:13 cannot be a new Bible?

Moon teaches that the tree of life talked about in Genesis 3 represents the perfected Adam. Read the verses in context and ask how could Adam eat of a symbolic image of himself?

There is only one name given for salvation on earth according to Acts 4:10-12. Surely this is the name of Jesus Christ and not Rev Moon?

The Bible clearly says that full salvation has already been accomplished, Colossians 1:13 and 1 Thessalonians 5:23. Jesus also said, 'It is finished' not 'I am finished' (John 19:30). What could Moon possibly add to the work that Jesus had already finished?

Our salvation is not of works, but totally of grace (Ephesians 2:8,9). Working then, produces nothing!

Clearly the cross of Christ was not a failure because from the beginning it was shown that he had to die. The Passover (Exodus 12) is an example of this as is the scapegoat of Leviticus 16. What were these events looking forward to? Surely, 'the Lamb of God who takes away the sin of the world' (John 1:29). Finally remember that without the shedding of blood there is no remission of sin (Hebrews 9:22).

What does the Bible teach about the return of the Messiah? Can it be used to show that Moon is the one? Acts 1:10-11 clearly shows that the way he left is the way he will return. Not born of a woman the second time! Matthew 24 and Revelation 1:7 both show that every eye will see him when he returns and Philippians 2 adds that every knee shall bow. It will not be a question of 'brainwashing' people to believe – they will know!

If you lose an argument do not worry. Sow doubt and share the truth of Scripture and the reality of Jesus with them. Make a loving but clear contrast between the life and words of Jesus and the life and words of Moon.

15

Christian Science

Where did they come from?

The founder of Christian Science was Mary Baker Eddy. Born in 1821, the youngest of six children, she lived on a farm in the state of New Hampshire, USA. Her religious upbringing was that of a Congregationalist but during her teenage years she rejected their strong Calvinistic teachings.

Christian Science in many ways owes its existence to Mary's often poor health. This state is said to have caused her to question why the healings of Jesus were not manifest in her day. Seeking to find a human cure she was to experiment with homeopathy and hypnotism among other alternatives but nothing seemed to work.

Mary was first married when she was 22 but sadly her husband died after only seven months. The second marriage lasted longer but eventually it ended in divorce. Her third attempt at marriage was in 1877 to Asa Eddy who was to be her first disciple in Christian Science. However, it was during her second marriage in 1862 that she visited Phineas Quimby to find relief from her spinal illness. Quimby, who was to be involved in starting other cults such as Unity, used hypnosis and autosuggestion to bring healing. The man and his methods made an obvious impression on Mary and at one point she wrote to a local newspaper comparing Quimby to Jesus Christ.

Where the Church started

In 1866 she claimed healing from a serious injury that she was to declare later left her with only three days to live. The story goes that she was miraculously cured after reading Matthew 9:1-8 especially verse 2, 'And behold, they were bringing to him a paralytic, lying on a bed; and Jesus seeing their faith said to the paralytic, "Take courage, my son, your sins are forgiven."'

Looking back on the event it was not the physical healing that took on most significance. Rather, it was the awareness that she had received revelation of spiritual truths she had long searched for. She began to study for long hours and this led eventually in 1875 to her first publication, *Science and Health – with Key to the Scriptures*. Fifteen other writings would follow before her death. She claimed that *Science and Health* was her original study and that God was its author.

I would blush to write of *Science and Health – with Key to the Scriptures* as I have, were it of human origin and apart from God its author, but as I was only a scribe echoing the harmonies of Heaven in divine metaphysics, I cannot be super-modest of the Christian Science textbook (*Christian Science Journal*, January 1901).

However, there is some proof that it was taken from other sources such as Phineas Quimby and a German-American philosopher, Francis Lieber.

The first Christian Science church was founded in Boston, Mass, USA, on 12 April 1879. Today there are some 2,500 branches in 68 countries governed by the *Manual of the Mother Church* first published in 1895.

Coming to the present day

Science and Health has now been translated into eighteen different languages and has been joined by regular publications, such as the *Christian Science Journal* that was first published in 1883. The *Christian Science Quarterly* came next in 1890 and then in 1898 the *Christian Science Sentinel* appeared. Many will also be aware of their newspaper, *The Christian Science Monitor*, which was first published in 1908. It has a daily edition in the USA and a weekly edition in 147 other countries. Apart from the written word Christian Science has also over the years broadcast several radio and television programmes especially in the USA.

Financial problems

Modern-day financial problems have meant certain cutbacks and their monthly magazine *World Monitor* ceased to be pub-lished in May 1993. The project had only lasted five years and closed with reported losses of $36.5 million. This closure came on top of the cancellation of its cable television network.

The Annual General Meeting held on 8 June 1992 was dom-inated by two interrelated financial matters. First, the closure of the television cable channel at a cost of $68.5 million and second, the publication of a controversial book. Their president Nathan Talbot was aware of the problems when he told the assembly, 'There are issues that would try and divide us. But . . . the practice of spiritual healing binds us together'.

Clearly there was a crisis among the Christian Scientists. The roots of this crisis could be found in the financial situation because they were losing $6,000,000 every month. This led on to an even deeper crisis of conscience.

Under the terms of a 1972 will, the church could inherit $97,000,000 if it published a book, *The Destiny of the Mother Church*, by Bliss Knapp, before April 1993. The problem was that many Christian Scientists believed that the book was heretical. They felt that it came very close to teaching that Mary Baker Eddy was a second Christ. She was described as God's, 'original woman', and Jesus was God's, 'original man'. Whatever the struggle of conscience the financial needs won and the book has now been published. The matter does not seem to be finished, though, as some Christian Scientists are now suing those who allowed the book to be published.

At headquarters all are not happy about this and several top officials have been banished from the church's Boston centre, security guards barring their entrance. It remains to be seen what lasting damage will be caused to Christian Science by the publishing of the book and the ejecting of these senior members.

Who are they?

Christian Science is reported to be losing ground in these days, with a 50% decline in practitioners in recent years. According to their own records most of the members these days are American women.

Christian Science is *neither* Christian nor scientific. The central theme of its teachings is healing but with little scope for doctors or hospitals. Their philosophy is based on a mind over matter mentality. Many will sadly struggle with their illnesses and there are reported cases of tragic deaths because medical treatment is refused. I wonder how these people would react if they knew that Mary Baker Eddy in her lifetime could never prove one healing. She even had to turn to doctors at the end of her life, for a regular supply of morphine. Eddy indeed is the 'dying' proof that Christian Science is a fake. However, many who believe today will feel that they have a testimony of being 'healed' through the message of Christian Science. They will not want to hear anything to the contrary and will passionately believe that there is no other way.

What do they believe?

The tenets of their faith, found in, *Christian Science: A Report for the 90s*, p. 79, need to be read closely, because at first glance some may appear Christian.

> 1. As adherents of Truth, we take the inspired Word of the Bible as our sufficient guide to eternal life.
>
> 2. We acknowledge and adore one supreme and infinite God. We acknowledge His Son, one Christ; the Holy Ghost or divine Comforter; and man in God's image and likeness.
>
> 3. We acknowledge God's forgiveness of sin in the destruction of sin and the spiritual understanding that casts out evil as unreal. But the belief in sin is punished so long as the belief lasts.
>
> 4. We acknowledge Jesus's atonement as the evidence of divine, efficacious Love, unfolding man's unity with God through Christ Jesus the Way-shower; and we acknowledge that man is saved through Christ, through Truth, Life and Love as demonstrated by the Galilean Prophet in healing the sick and overcoming sin and death.
>
> 5. We acknowledge that the crucifixion of Jesus and his resurrection served to uplift faith to understand eternal Life, even the allness of Soul, Spirit, and the nothingness of matter.
>
> 6. And we solemnly promise to watch, and pray for that Mind to be in us which was also in Christ Jesus, to do unto others as we would have them do unto us; and to be merciful, just, and pure.

Mary Baker Eddy's writings show that she believed that Christian Science was based on Scripture:

> The Bible has been my only authority. I have no other guide in 'the straight and narrow way' of Truth. *Science and Health*, p. 126.

She considered that her writings were inspired, 'No human pen nor tongue taught me the Science contained in this book' *Science and Health*, p. 110. It is therefore no surprise that Christian Science seeks to go beyond the Bible and restore what was lost. It puts its own meaning into the Scriptures as the Lord's Prayer with spiritual interpretation by Eddy shows.

> Our Father which art in heaven,
>> Our Father-Mother God, all harmonious.
> Hallowed be Thy name.
>> Adorable One.
> Thy kingdom come.
>> Thy kingdom is come; Thou art ever-present.
> Thy will be done in earth, as it is in heaven.
>> Enable us to know, – as in heaven, so on earth, – God is omnipotent, supreme.
> Give us this day our daily bread;
>> Give us grace for to-day; feed the famished affections;
> And forgive us our debts, as we forgive our debtors.
>> And Love is reflected in love;
> And lead us not into temptation, but deliver us from evil;
>> And God leadeth us not into temptation, but delivereth us from sin, disease, and death.
> For Thine is the kingdom, and the power, and the glory, forever.
>> For God is infinite, all-power, all Life, Truth, Love, over all, and All. (*Science and Health*, pp. 16–17 quoted in *Christian Science: A Report for the 90s*, p. 78.)

Their first tenet shows that they believe the Bible to be the *sufficient guide to eternal life*. But compare this with what Jesus said, 'You search the Scriptures, because you think that in them you have eternal life; and it is these that bear witness of me' John 5:39. However the report mentioned above, on page 40, shows clearly that Christian Scientists put *Science and*

Health above the King James Version of the Bible. *Science and Health* is the guide to the guide to eternal life and so more important.

> These two books serve as the Church's pastor . . . People hungering for a better understanding of the Bible – yearning to see how it applies to today's world and to their own lives – find insight in *Science and Health*.

Mary Baker Eddy tried to say that her **God** was not pantheistic, ie in everything, but her teaching shows the contrary.

> (God is) The great I Am; the all-knowing, all-seeing, all acting, all-wise, all-loving and eternal; Principle; Mind; Soul: Spirit; Life; Truth; Love; all Substance; Intelligence (*Science and Health*, p. 587).

This pantheistic God also is evident in the last line of her interpretation of the Lord's prayer shown above.

> *Christ* is the ideal Truth, that comes to heal sickness and sin through Christian Science. Jesus is the name of the man who, more than all other men, has presented Christ, the true idea of God (*Science and Health*, p. 473).

This 'Christ idea' or 'Christ consciousness' comes from eastern religions and appears in many New Age cults.

Eddy also makes it plain that Jesus is not God.

> Jesus Christ is not God, as Jesus himself declared, but is the Son of God (*Science and Health*, p. 361).

She further claims that Jesus did not make full atonement for sin. Our effort is still needed.

Final deliverance from error . . . is not reached . . . by pinning one's faith without works to another's vicarious effort . . . One sacrifice, however great, is insufficient to pay the debt of sin. The atonement requires constant self-immolation on the sinner's part. That God's wrath should be vented upon His beloved Son, is divinely unnatural. Such a theory is man-made (*Science and Health*, pp. 22/23).

What is even more amazing is that Eddy goes on to tell us that Jesus did not really die!

His disciples believed Jesus to be dead while he was hidden in the sepulchre, whereas he was alive, demonstrating within the narrow tomb the power of the Spirit to overrule mortal, material sense (*Science and Health*, p. 44).

The cornerstone of Christian Science is **healing** and they alone have discovered the secret of Jesus' healing ministry.

Our Master . . . practised Christian healing . . . but left no definite rule for demonstrating this Principle of healing and preventing disease. This rule remained to be discovered by Christian Science (*Science and Healing*, p. 147).

Many testimonies are published in various Christian Scientist magazines claiming miraculous recovery from illness. Some would appear genuine and this should not surprise us. The test of something is not whether it works but where it comes from. There may be a 'power' in some of Christian Science but it certainly does not come from God as their beliefs clearly show. They have another Jesus and another gospel.

Sin, sickness, death and hell are all unreal to the Christian Scientist. Salvation comes not from a relationship with Jesus Christ but from pretending the evil is not real. Hell is only the bad things within us and the effects of sin. (See *Science and Health*, p. 588.)

> . . . the only reality of sin, sickness, or death is the awful fact that unrealities seem real to human, erring belief, until God strips off their disguise (*Science and Health*, p. 472).

Most likely meeting points

Apart from friends and neighbours the presence of Christian Scientists is seen from their large church buildings and reading rooms. Many looking for help will drop into these rooms. They do, of course, still have several regular publications and these too can often be found in doctors' waiting rooms, etc.

Sharing the gospel

We have already mentioned the supposed belief of the Christian Scientist, 'As adherents of Truth, we take the inspired Word of the Bible as our sufficient guide to eternal Life'. *Science and Health*, p. 497.

This is a good place to start because if the Bible is the guide to eternal life, Mary Baker Eddy is the guide to hell. Ask them to compare the teachings of Eddy with the teachings of the Bible and choose which one to believe. Ask them why, if the Bible is the guide to eternal life, Eddy's beliefs are so different. Why indeed, when in some areas they are going in the opposite direction. Would that not mean that if we followed those beliefs we too would be going in the opposite direction to eternal life?

Some subjects that would be especially good to discuss are listed here with appropriate references.

The Bible clearly speaks of the reality of sin, Romans 3:23 and 1 John 1:8-10.

The Bible shows the awful reality of Christ dying for the

penalty of our sin, 2 Corinthians 5:21, 1 Peter 2:24 and 1 John 2:2.

God is shown to be separate from his creation; all is not one, Isaiah 44:24 and Acts 17:24-25.

Jesus and the Christ are shown to be the same person, Luke 2:11, 1 John 2:22 and 1 John 5:1.

Jesus both claimed to be and accepted the claim that he was God, John 5:18 and 20:28.

The Gospel expressly includes the death of Christ, 1 Corinthians 15:3.

Conclusion

What do you do when you come to the end of a book like this? Put it on the shelf and forget it? Make a mental note that one day you must do something about it? I hope that you will not just put off the decision but be encouraged to put the lessons of this book into practice straight away.

There is a mission field waiting for you and it is not in some remote part of the globe. The challenge is of the cults on your doorstep or in your High Street. If you have had difficulty in getting people interested in the gospel in your area you should praise the Lord for the cults. Their members are not apathetic like so many you meet; most are already aware of their need for a spiritual input. We can šimply turn that to our advantage in communicating the gospel.

First, I am aware that I have not answered every question but as we are a ministry you are very welcome to write to us with further queries. Any subjects that we have raised that you do not understand or areas that are not clear please contact us at:

Reachout Trust
24 Ormond Road
Richmond
Surrey TW10 6TH

Phone: 0181 332 7786
Fax: 0181 332 0286

We may not be able to deal with every letter immediately but we will gladly answer any questions and provide further literature specifically designed to help you be ready to reach out to the cults in your area.

Second, I want to give you just a few ideas of what you can do so that you will not be just a hearer but a doer also.

You can be what I call a passive witness. This is where you take the lessons of this book to heart and get prepared. Then when the knock comes on the door or you meet the cult member in the High Street you spring into action. I pray that everyone who reads this book will at least go as far as that.

I am hoping that a number will take this further and become active witnesses. Here, we will not be just waiting for the cult members to come to us but will be looking for ways to contact them directly. Possibilities for achieving this are advertisements in shop windows, newspapers etc. It will mean that you will not only contact those in the cults but also those beginning to study with them. People in the latter category are very important because prevention is better than cure. In other words it is easier to show people it is wrong to go into the cult than to try to bring them out after many years. Hardly a week goes by at the office without two or three people of this kind contacting us. What is even better is that many find the true Saviour instead of the false gospel of the cults.

Another way that you can reach out is by arranging to deliver warning tracts in your neighbourhood. Beyond this you may want to be available to help others in the churches in your area to be ready to share their faith with cult members.

At Reachout Trust we want to hear from you, whatever your decision is concerning the message in this book. We would very much like to know what your conclusions are and why you have arrived at them because this will help us in our future work.

Finally, I want to say again that I hope that many of you will be encouraged and motivated to build bridges of love to those in the cults that are all around you and that we are here to help you in whatever way we can.